DEATH
THREAT

DEATH THREAT

VIVEK SHRAYA + NESS LEE

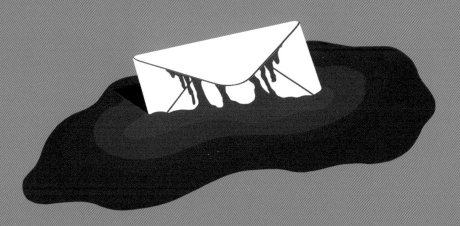

COLOURING BY
EMMETT PHAN + HIENG TANG

ARSENAL PULP PRESS
VANCOUVER

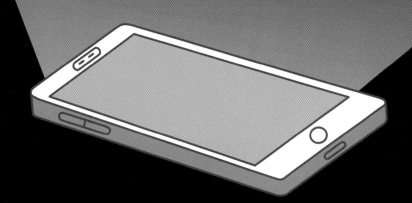
YOU HUNTED ME DOWN.

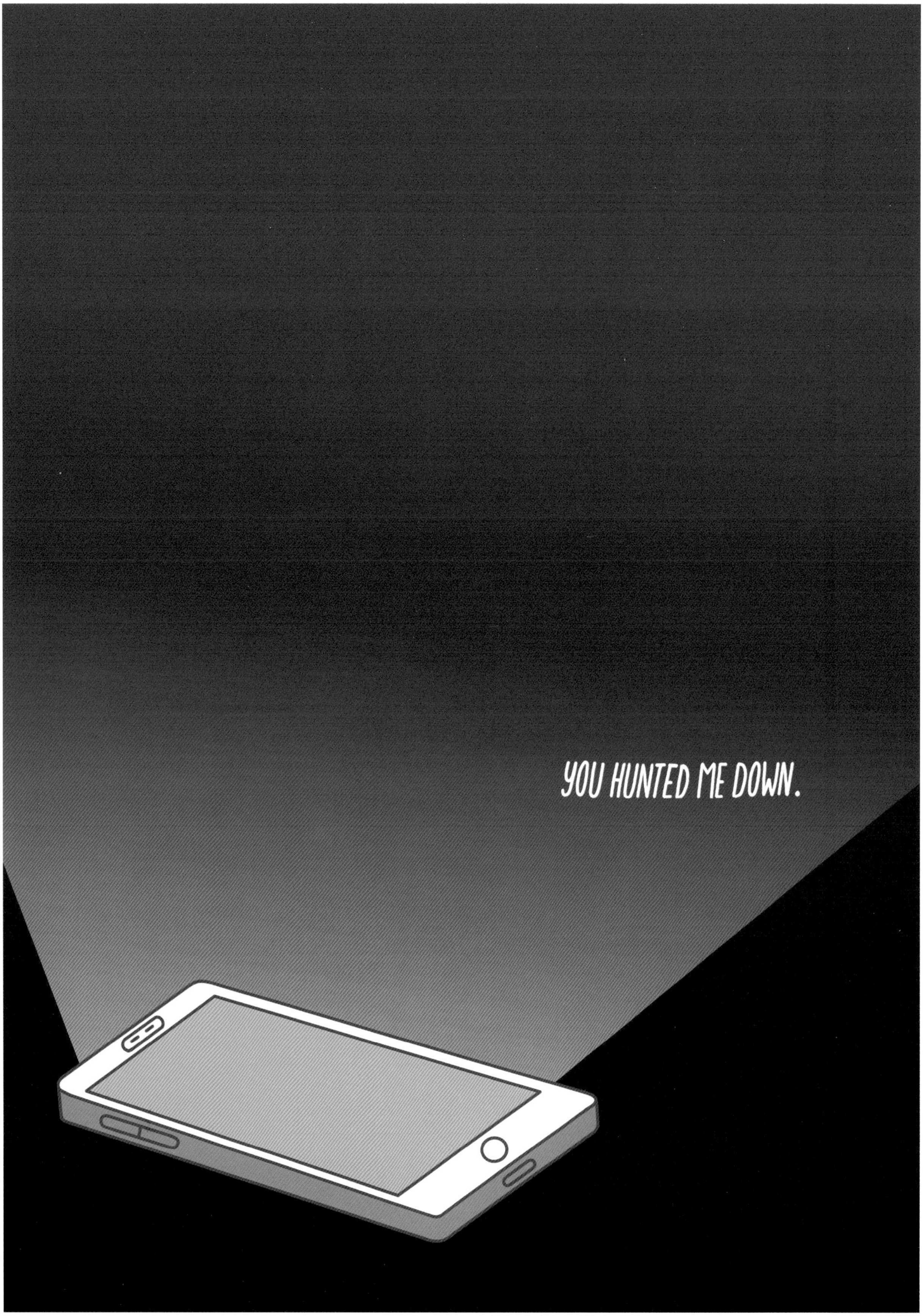

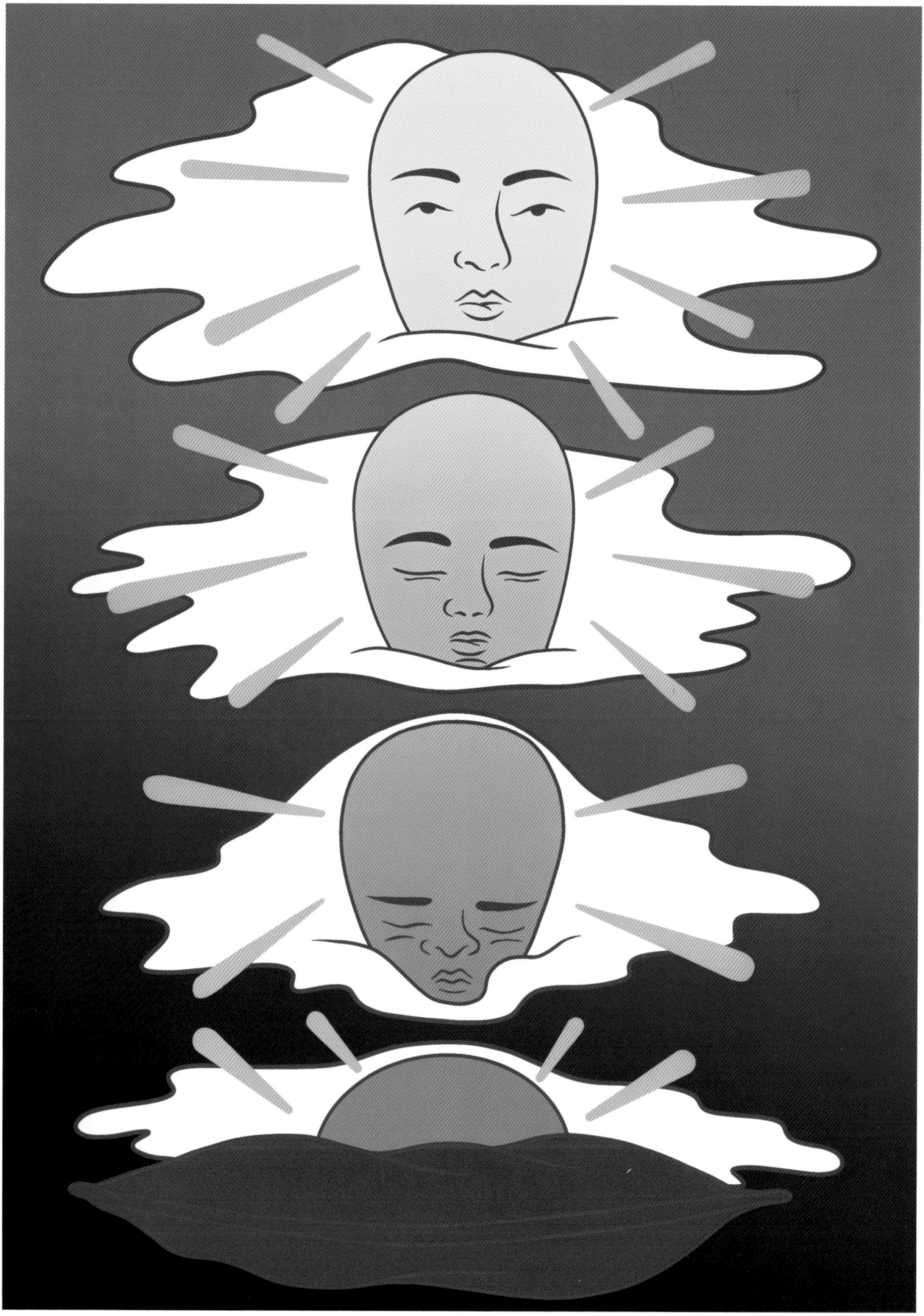

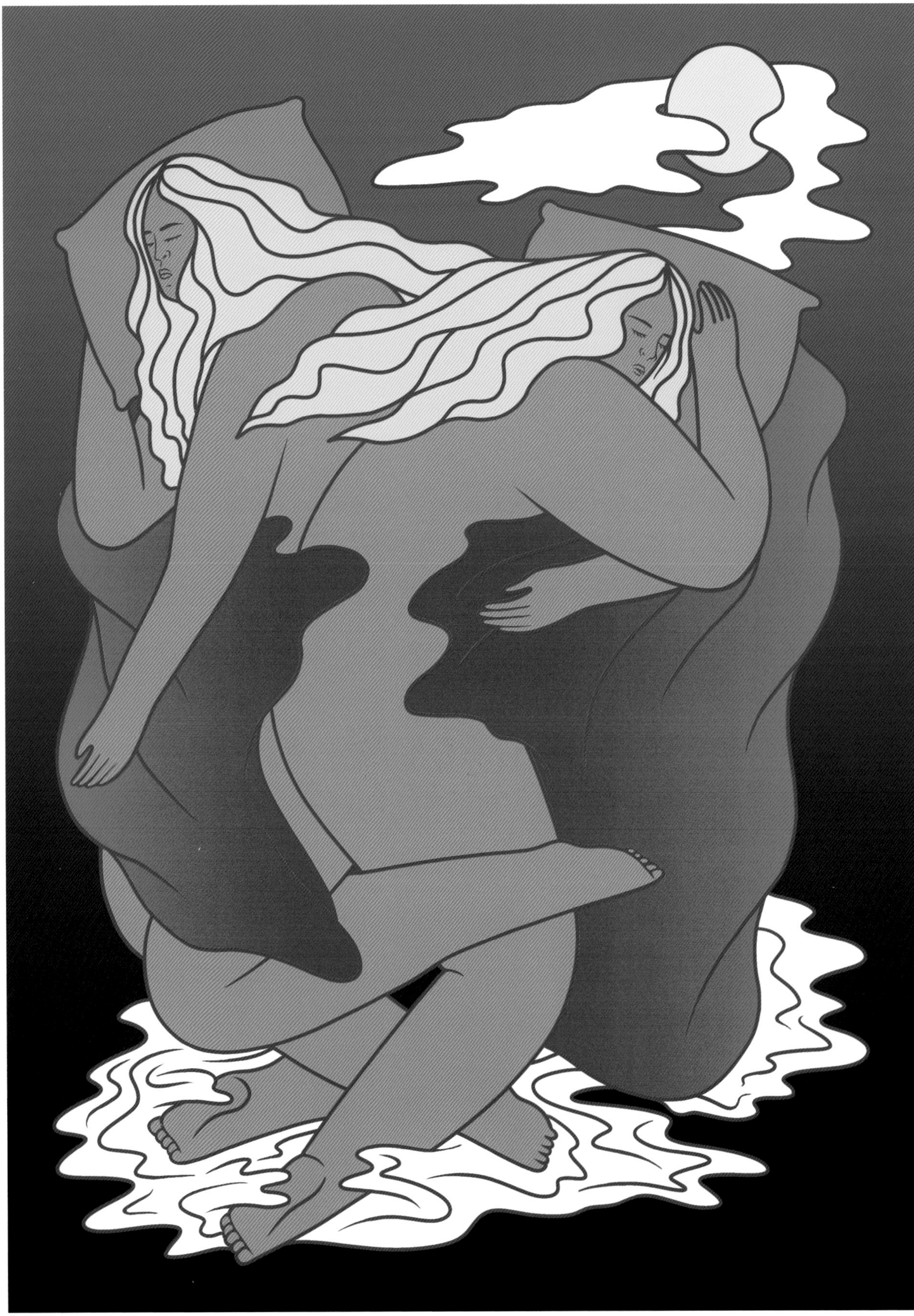

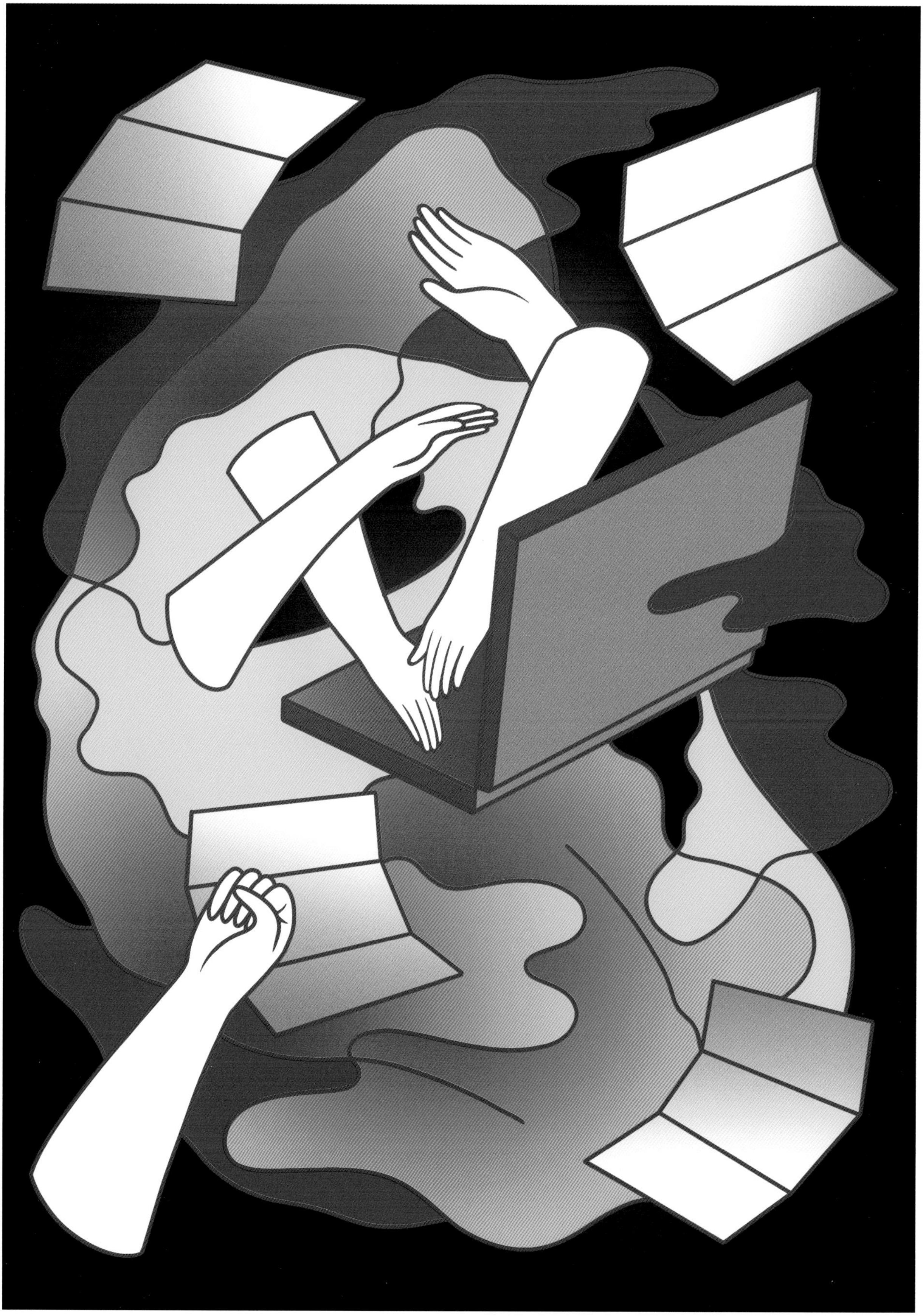

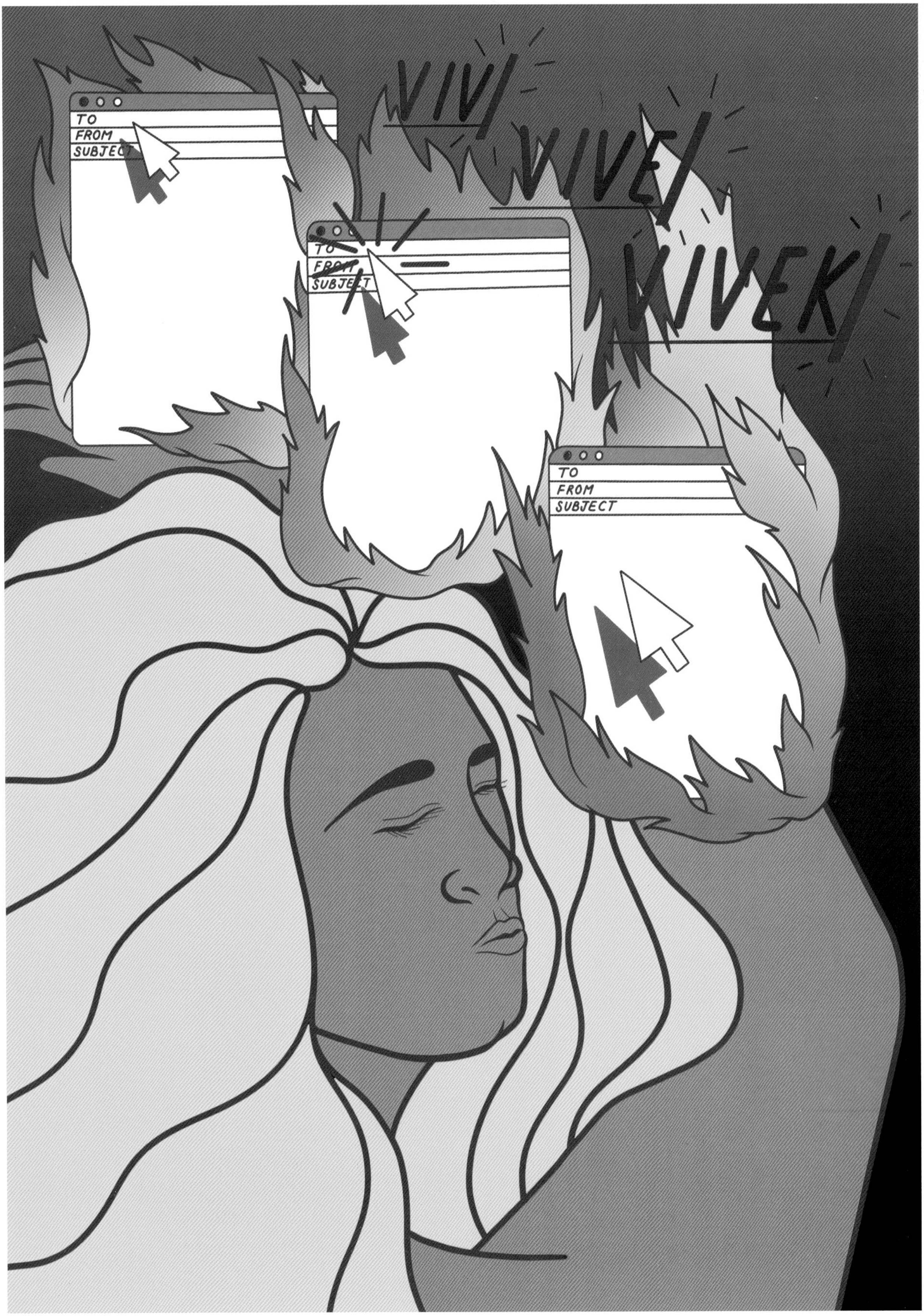
TO
FROM
SUBJECT
VIVI
VIVE
VIVEK
TO
FROM
SUBJECT

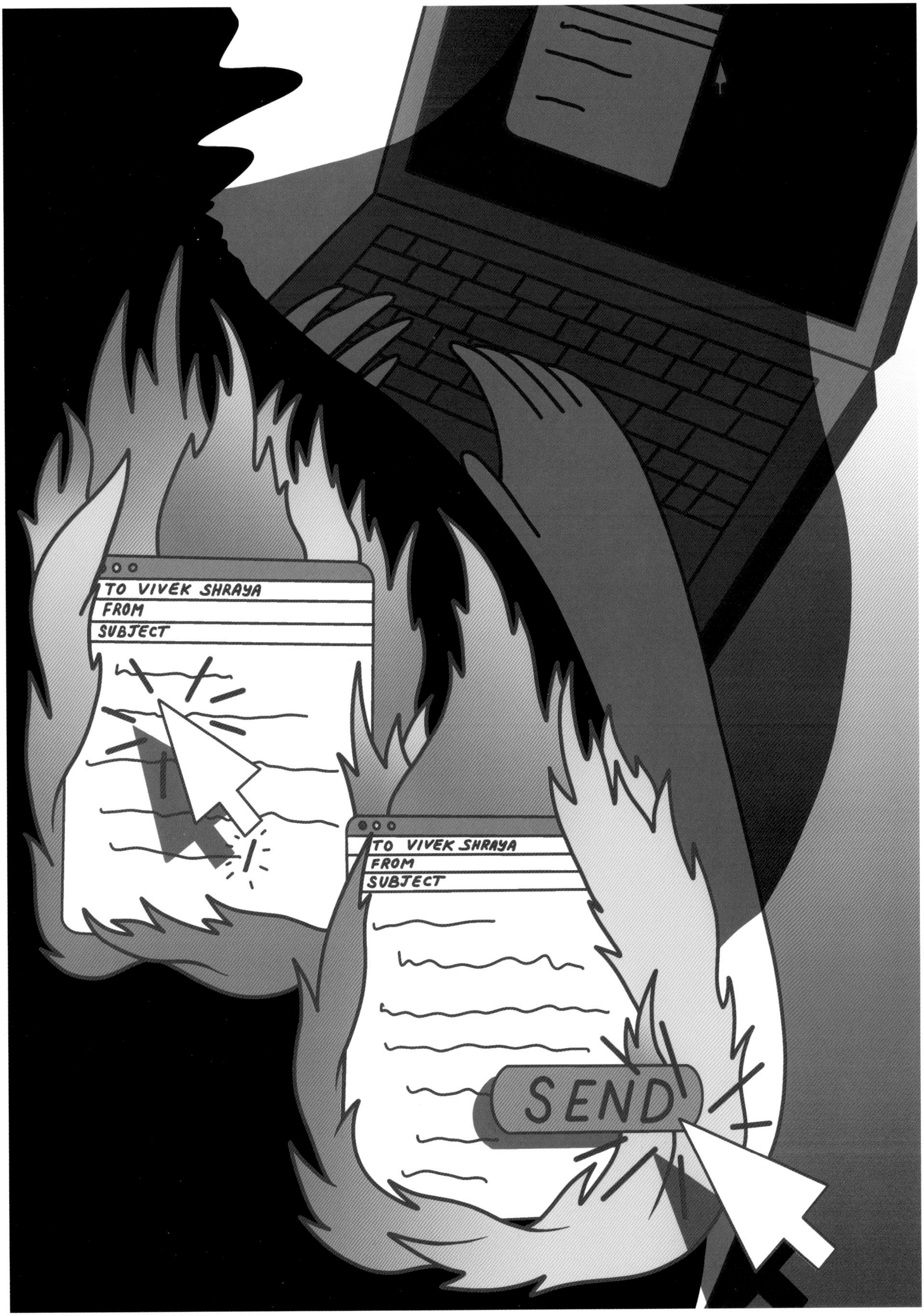
TO VIVEK SHRAYA
FROM
SUBJECT
TO VIVEK SHRAYA
FROM
SUBJECT
SEND

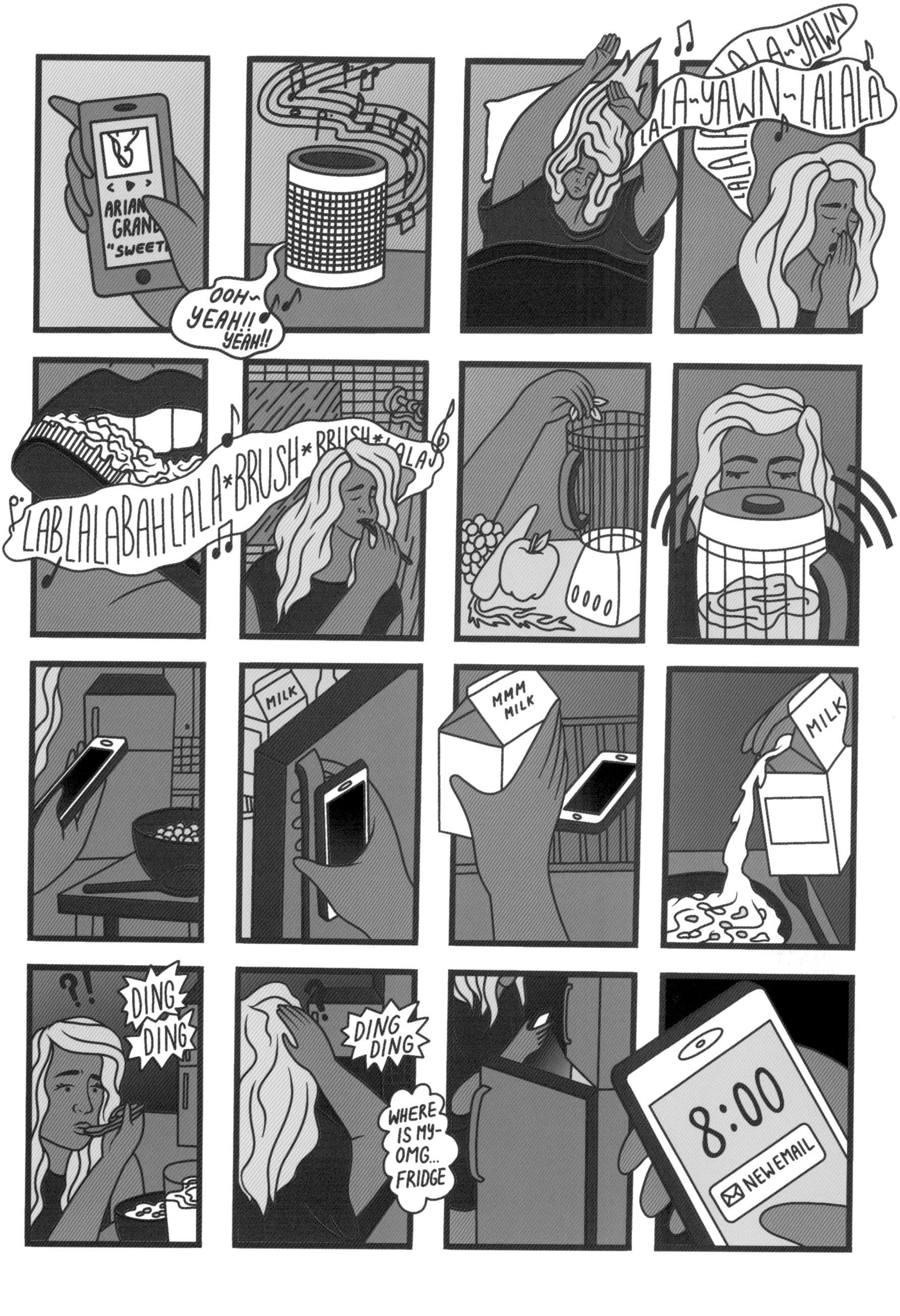
ARIANA GRAND
"SWEET
OOH~ YEAH!! YEAH!!
LALA~YAWN~LALALA~YAWN
LALALA
LABLALABAHLALA*BRUSH*BRUSH*LALA
MILK
MMM MILK
MILK
?!
DING DING
DING DING
WHERE IS MY- OMG... FRIDGE
8:00
NEW EMAIL

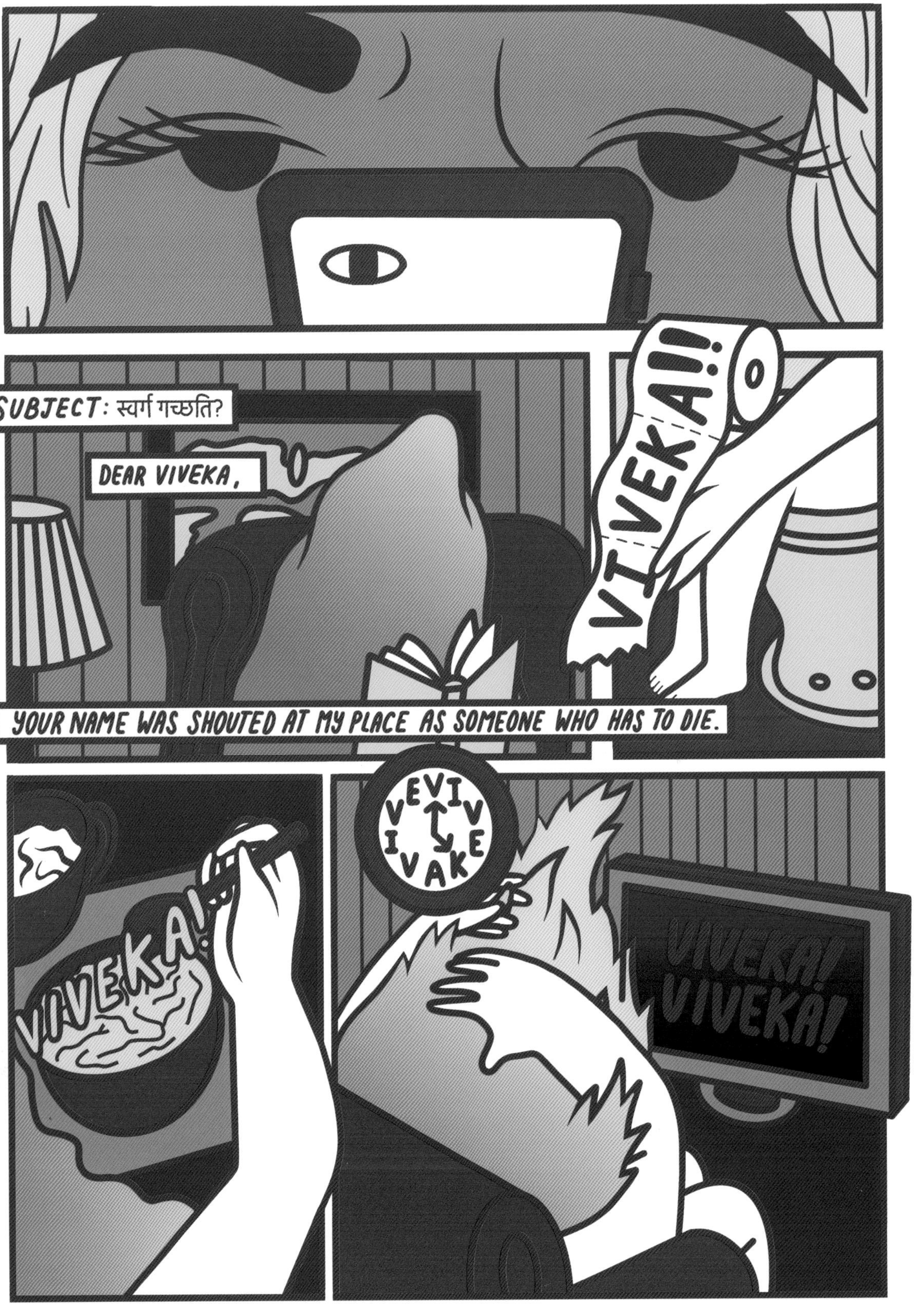
SUBJECT: स्वर्ग गच्छति?
DEAR VIVEKA,
VIVEKA!!
YOUR NAME WAS SHOUTED AT MY PLACE AS SOMEONE WHO HAS TO DIE.
VIVEKA!
VIVEKA!
VIVEKA!

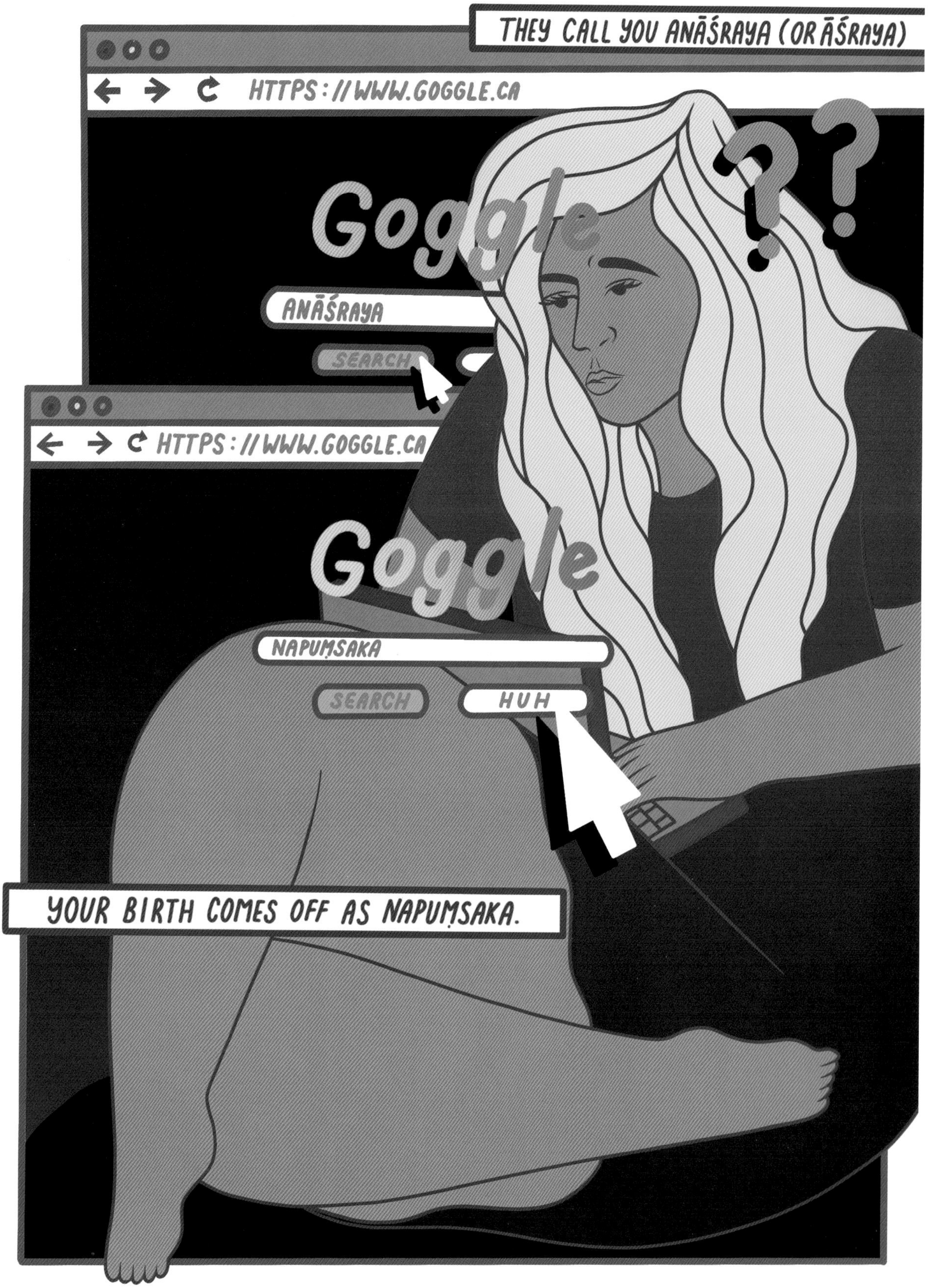
THEY CALL YOU ANĀŚRAYA (OR ĀŚRAYA)
HTTPS://WWW.GOGGLE.CA
Goggle
ANĀŚRAYA
SEARCH
HTTPS://WWW.GOGGLE.CA
Goggle
NAPUṂSAKA
SEARCH
HUH
YOUR BIRTH COMES OFF AS NAPUṂSAKA.

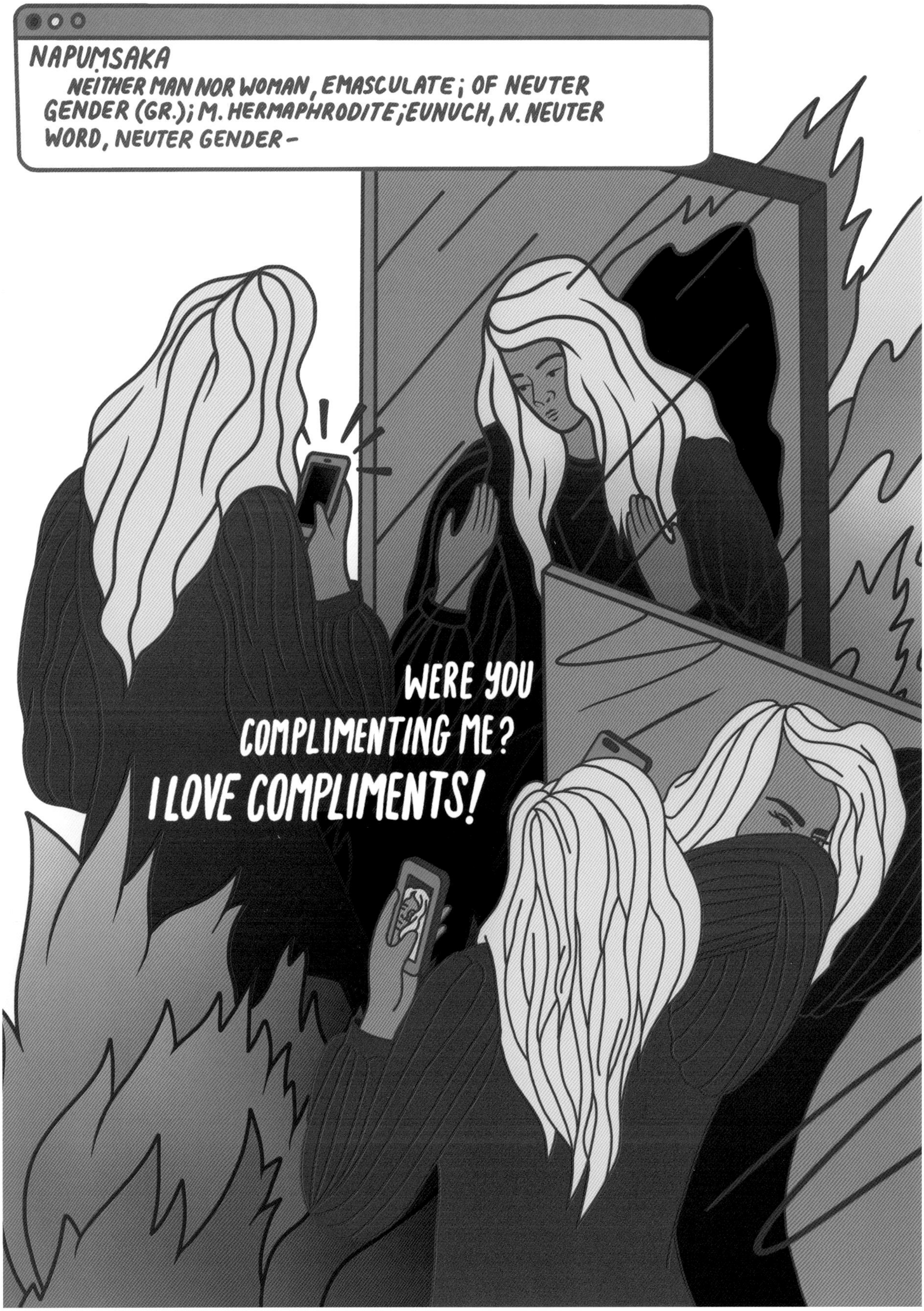
NAPUṂSAKA
NEITHER MAN NOR WOMAN, EMASCULATE; OF NEUTER GENDER (GR.); M. HERMAPHRODITE; EUNUCH, N. NEUTER WORD, NEUTER GENDER -
WERE YOU COMPLIMENTING ME? I LOVE COMPLIMENTS!

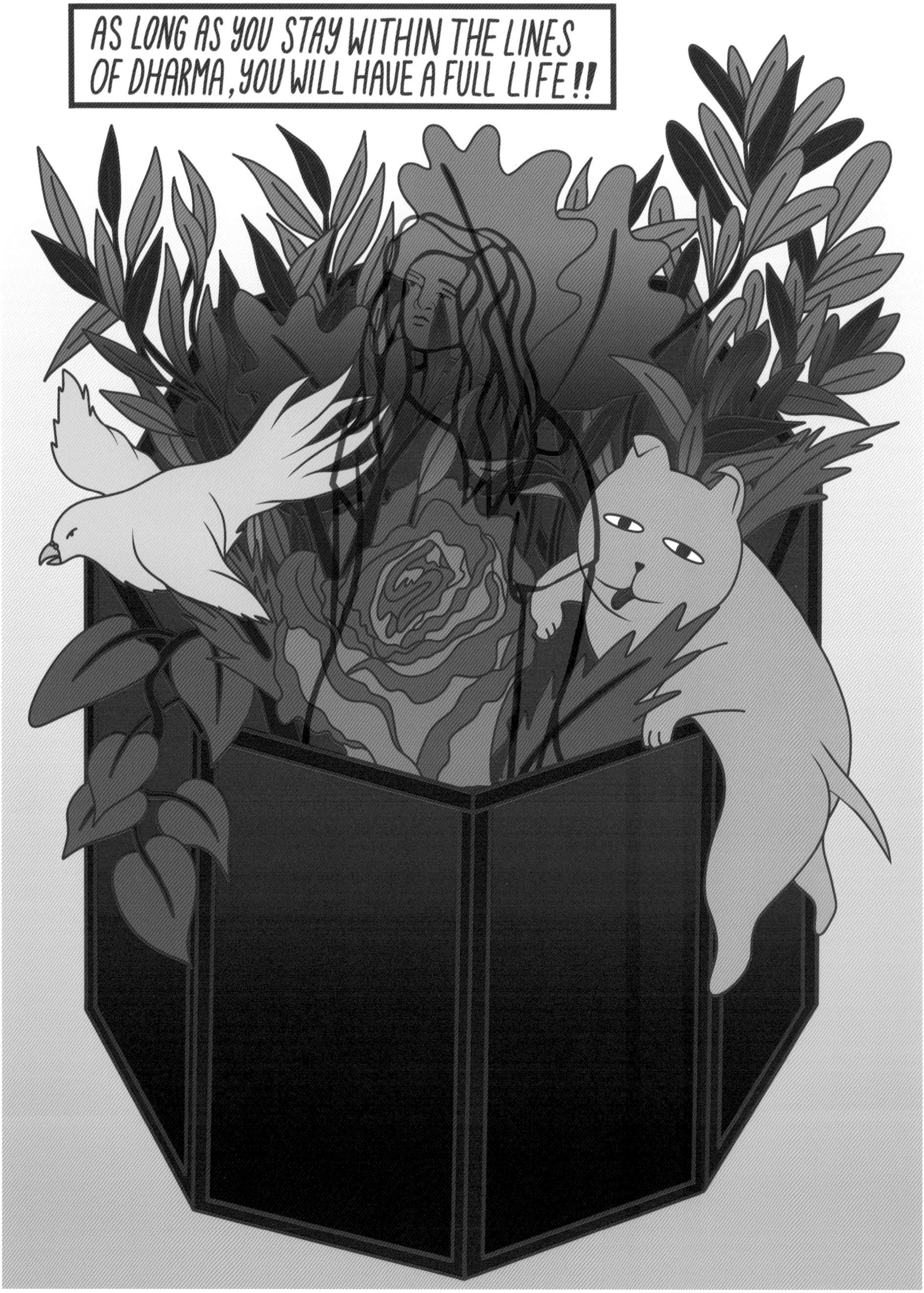
AS LONG AS YOU STAY WITHIN THE LINES OF DHARMA, YOU WILL HAVE A FULL LIFE!!

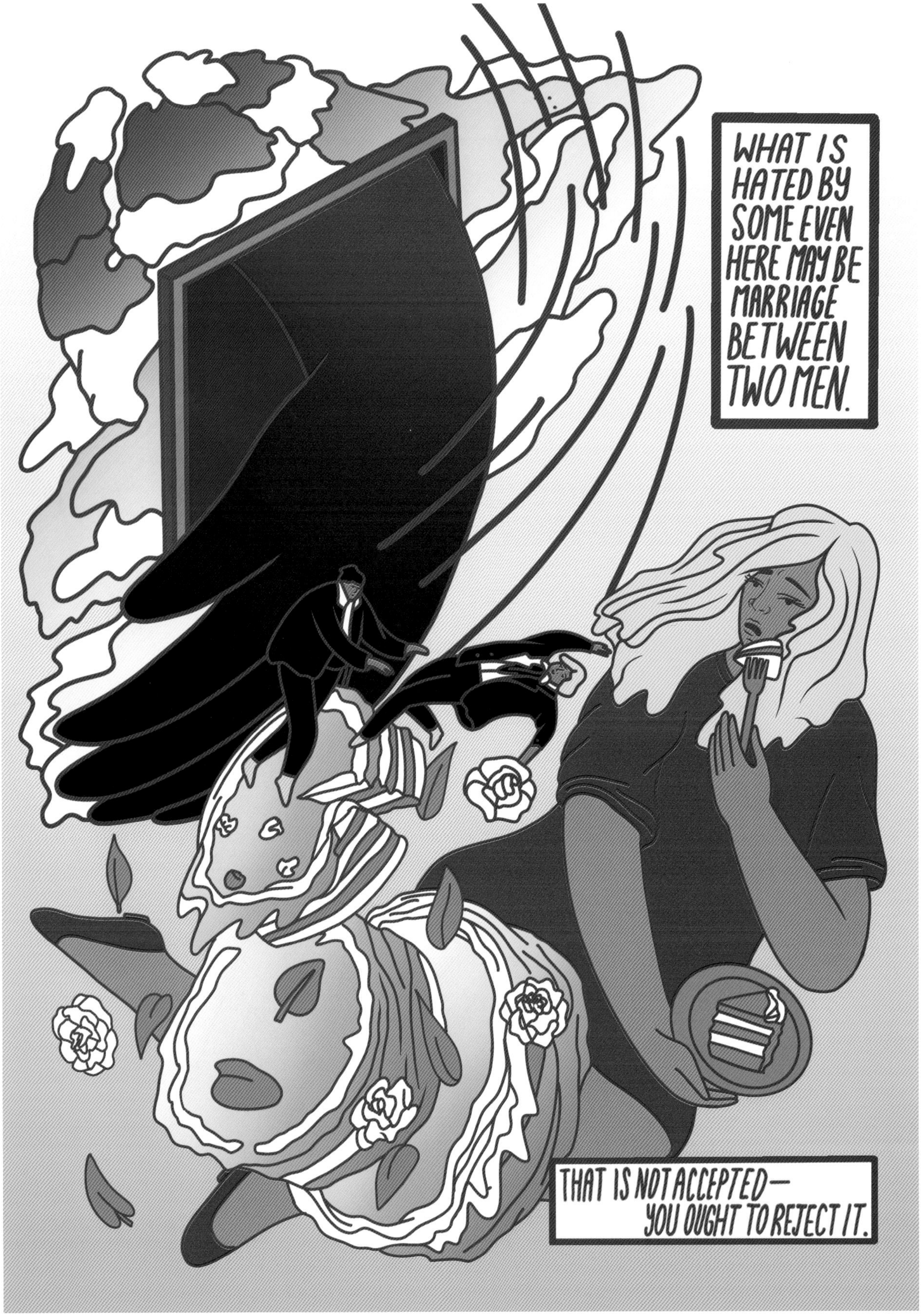
WHAT IS HATED BY SOME EVEN HERE MAY BE MARRIAGE BETWEEN TWO MEN.
THAT IS NOT ACCEPTED— YOU OUGHT TO REJECT IT.

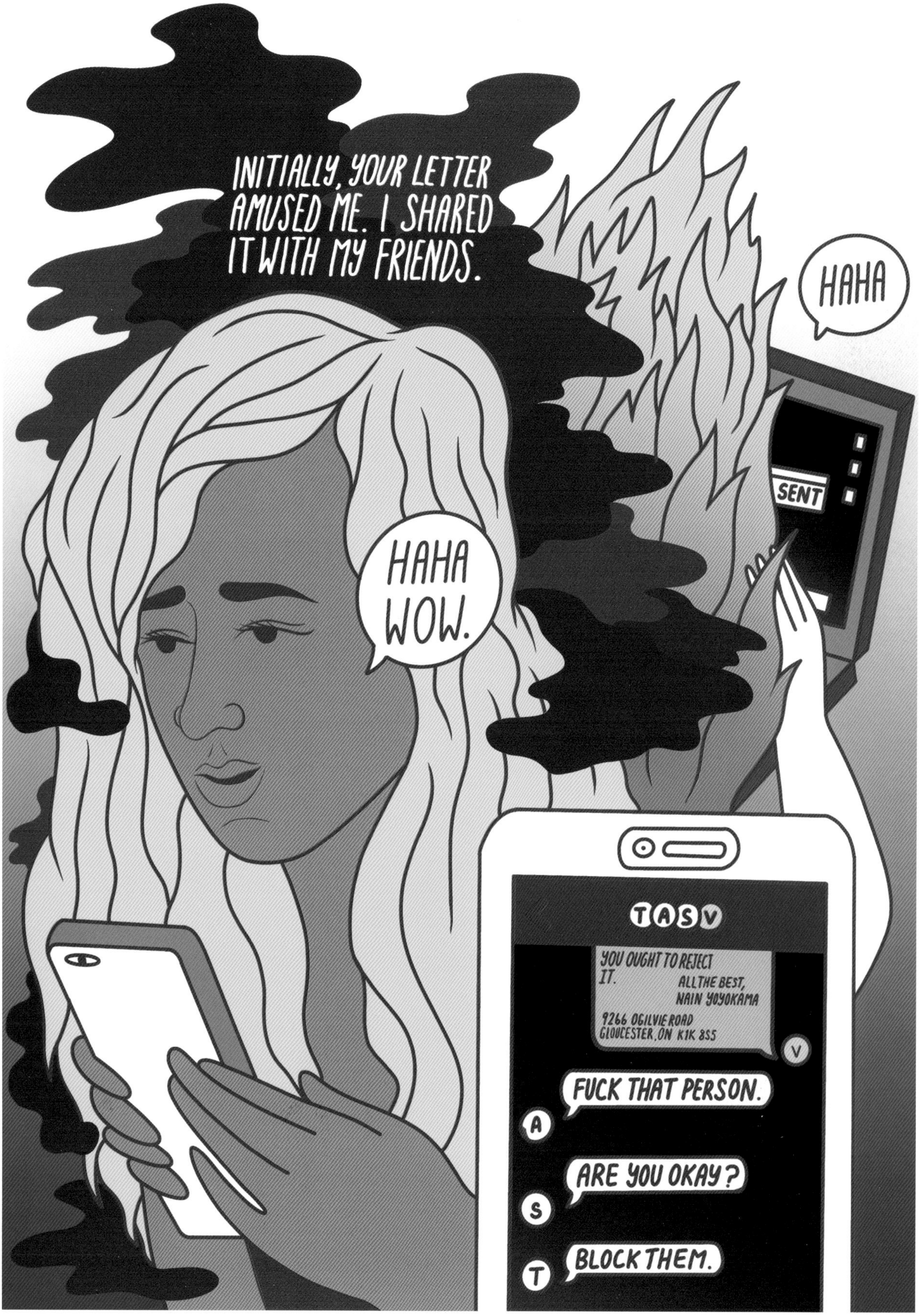
INITIALLY, YOUR LETTER AMUSED ME. I SHARED IT WITH MY FRIENDS.
HAHA
HAHA WOW.
SENT
TASV
YOU OUGHT TO REJECT IT. ALL THE BEST, NAIN YOYOKAMA
9266 OGILVIE ROAD GLOUCESTER, ON K1K 8S5
V
FUCK THAT PERSON.
A
ARE YOU OKAY?
S
BLOCK THEM.
T

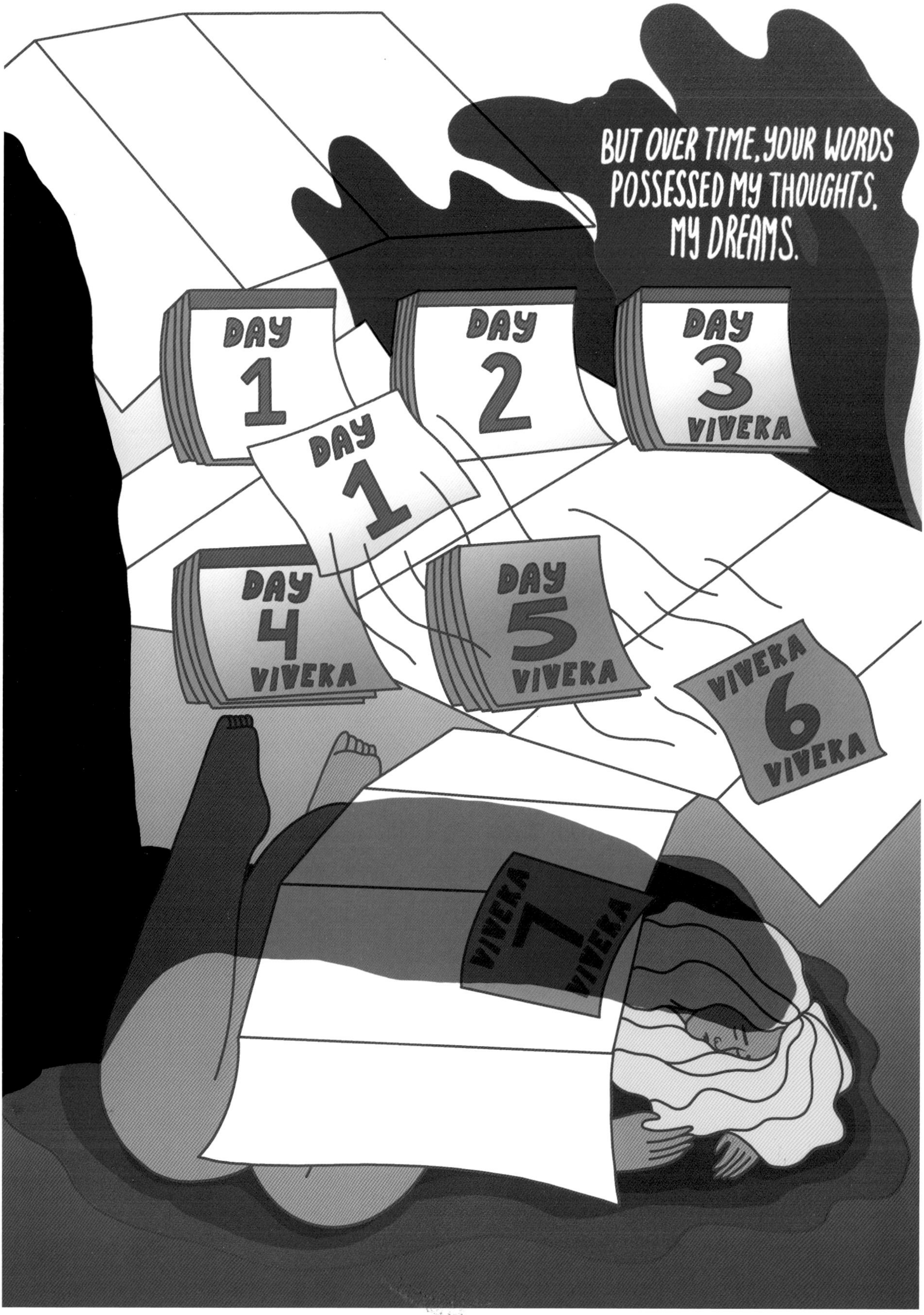
BUT OVER TIME, YOUR WORDS POSSESSED MY THOUGHTS. MY DREAMS.
DAY 1
DAY 2
DAY 3 VIVEKA
DAY 1
DAY 4 VIVEKA
DAY 5 VIVEKA
VIVEKA 6 VIVEKA
VIVEKA 7 VIVEKA

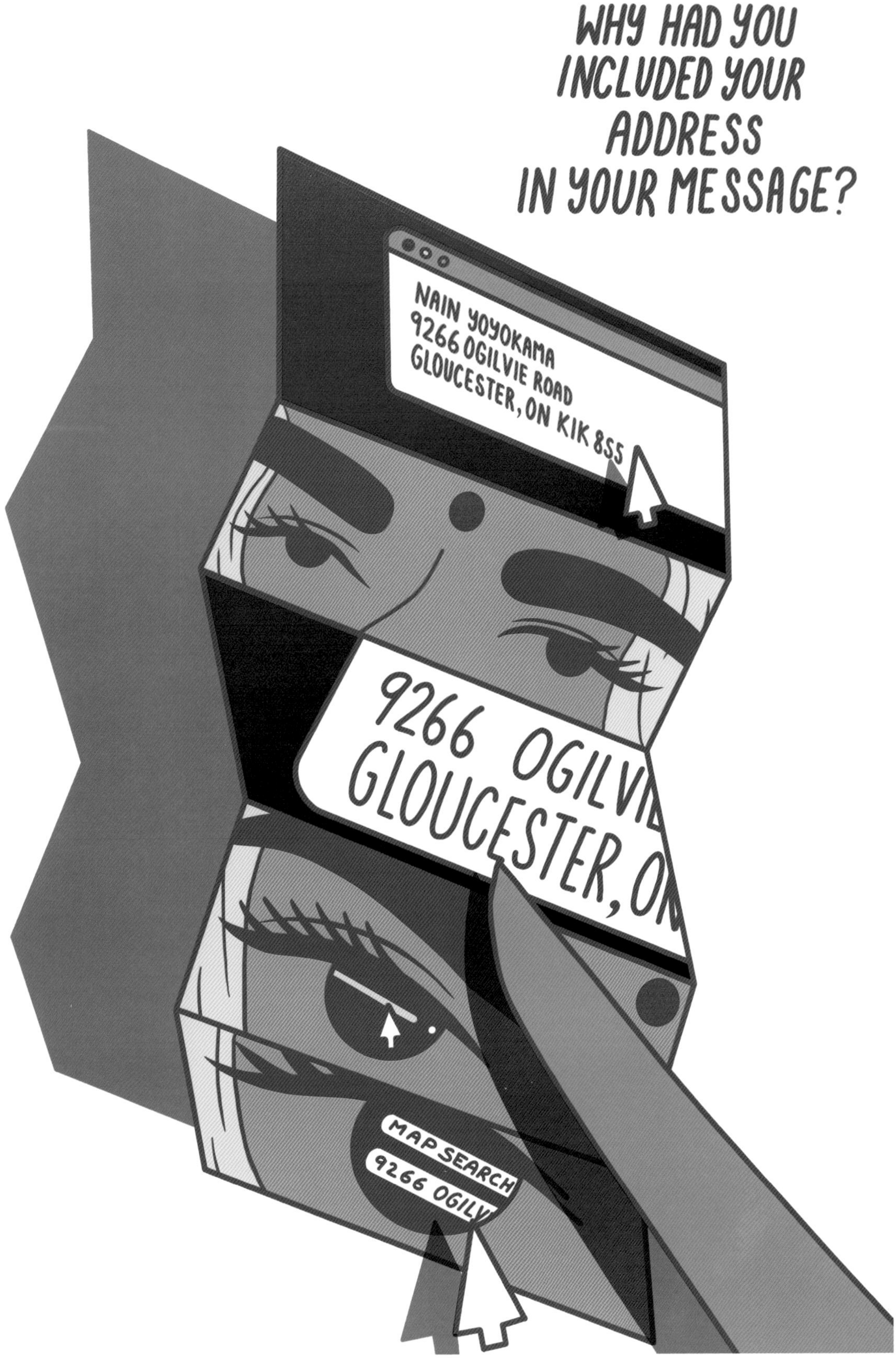
WHY HAD YOU INCLUDED YOUR ADDRESS IN YOUR MESSAGE?
NAIN YOYOKAMA
9266 OGILVIE ROAD
GLOUCESTER, ON KIK 8S5
MAP SEARCH

DID YOU WANT ME
TO HUNT YOU DOWN?

DID YOU WANT ME
TO COME OVER
FOR GAMES
NIGHT?

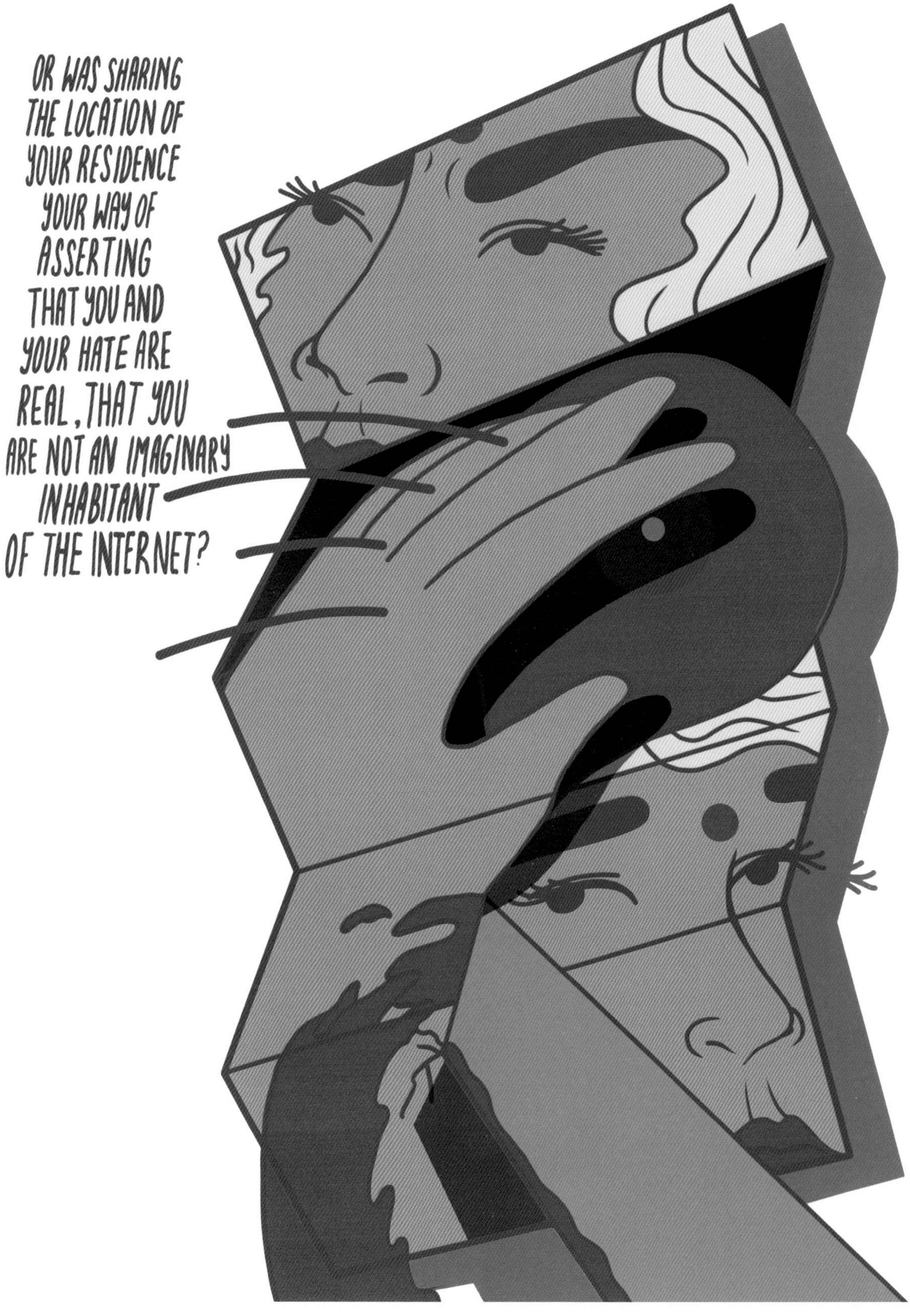
OR WAS SHARING THE LOCATION OF YOUR RESIDENCE YOUR WAY OF ASSERTING THAT YOU AND YOUR HATE ARE REAL, THAT YOU ARE NOT AN IMAGINARY INHABITANT OF THE INTERNET?

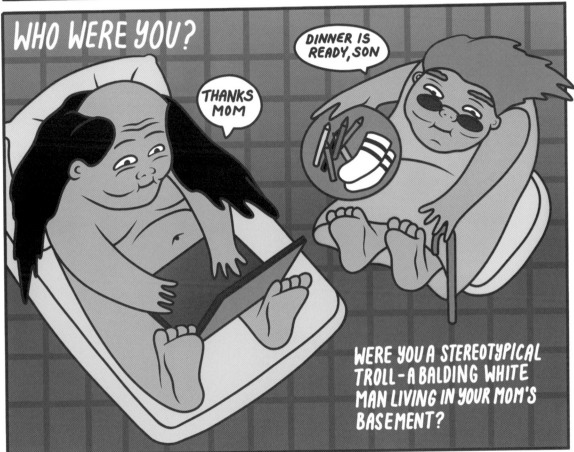

WHO WERE YOU?

THANKS MOM

DINNER IS READY, SON

WERE YOU A STEREOTYPICAL TROLL—A BALDING WHITE MAN LIVING IN YOUR MOM'S BASEMENT?

A BARISTA?   A PROFESSIONAL CLOWN?   A MASTER CHEF?   A GRAD STUDENT?   A BANKER?   A DOCTOR?

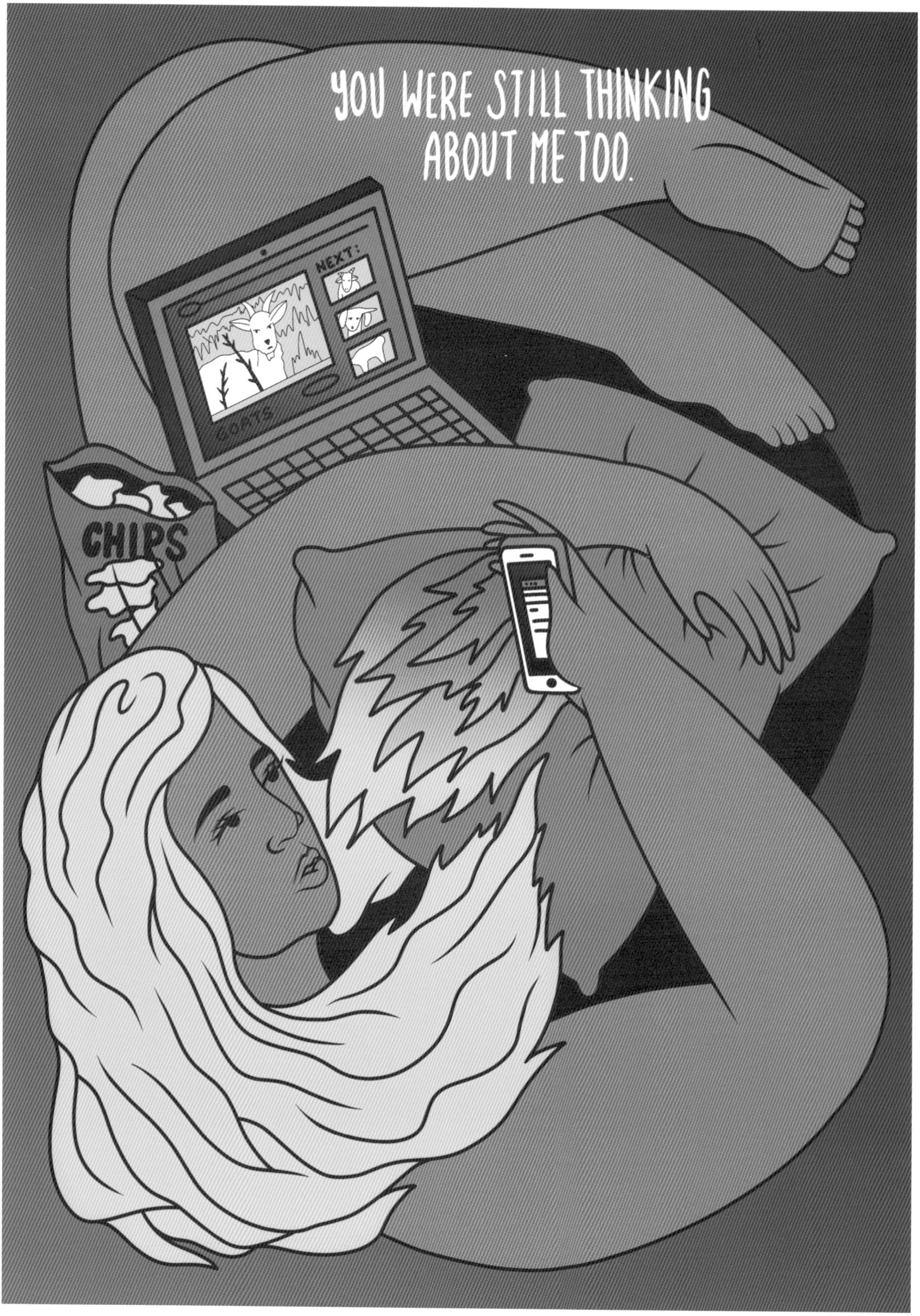
YOU WERE STILL THINKING
ABOUT ME TOO.
NEXT:
GOATS
CHIPS

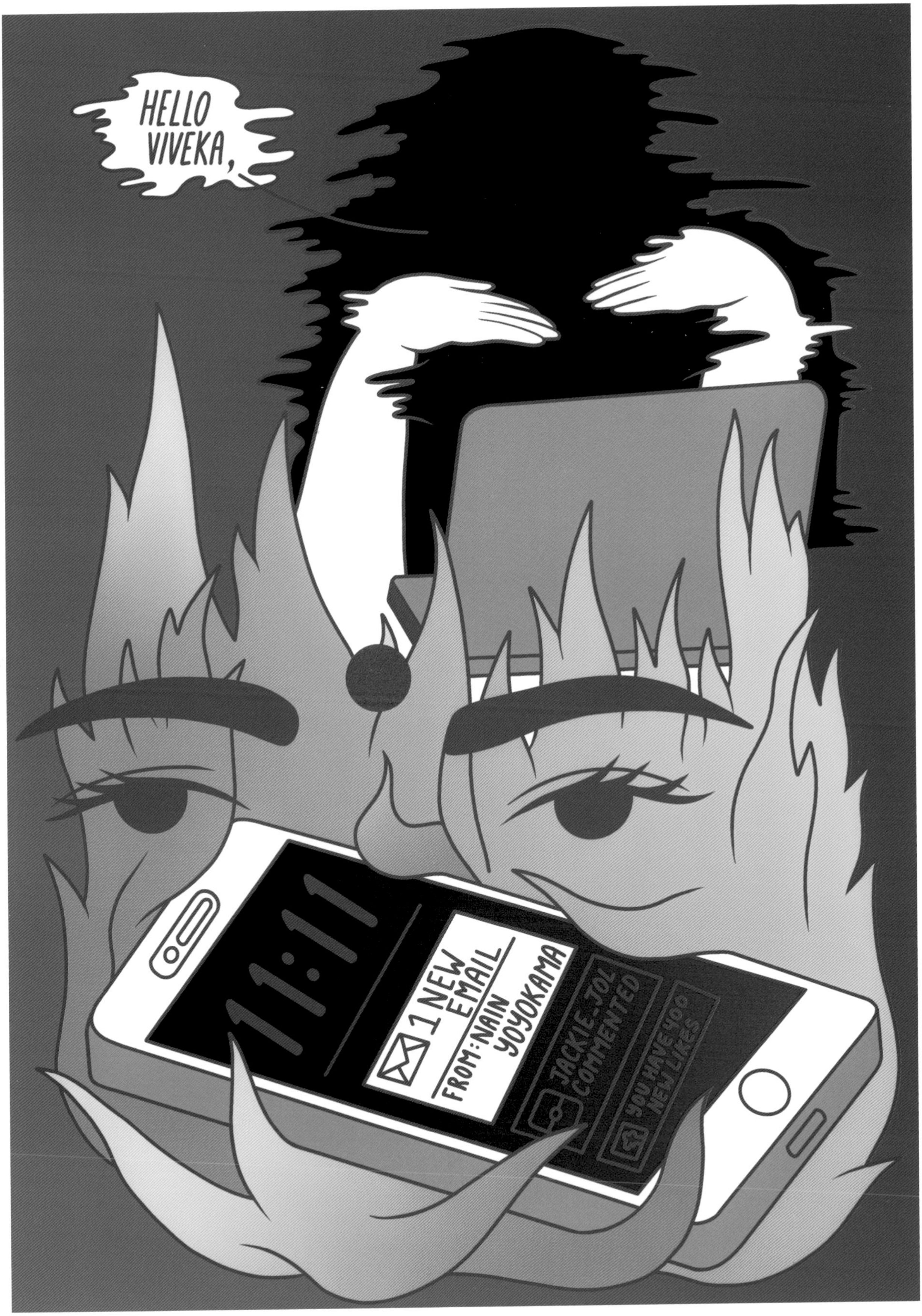
HELLO VIVEKA,
11:11
1 NEW EMAIL
FROM: NAIN YOYOKAMA
JACKIE-JOL COMMENTED
YOU HAVE 400 NEW LIKES

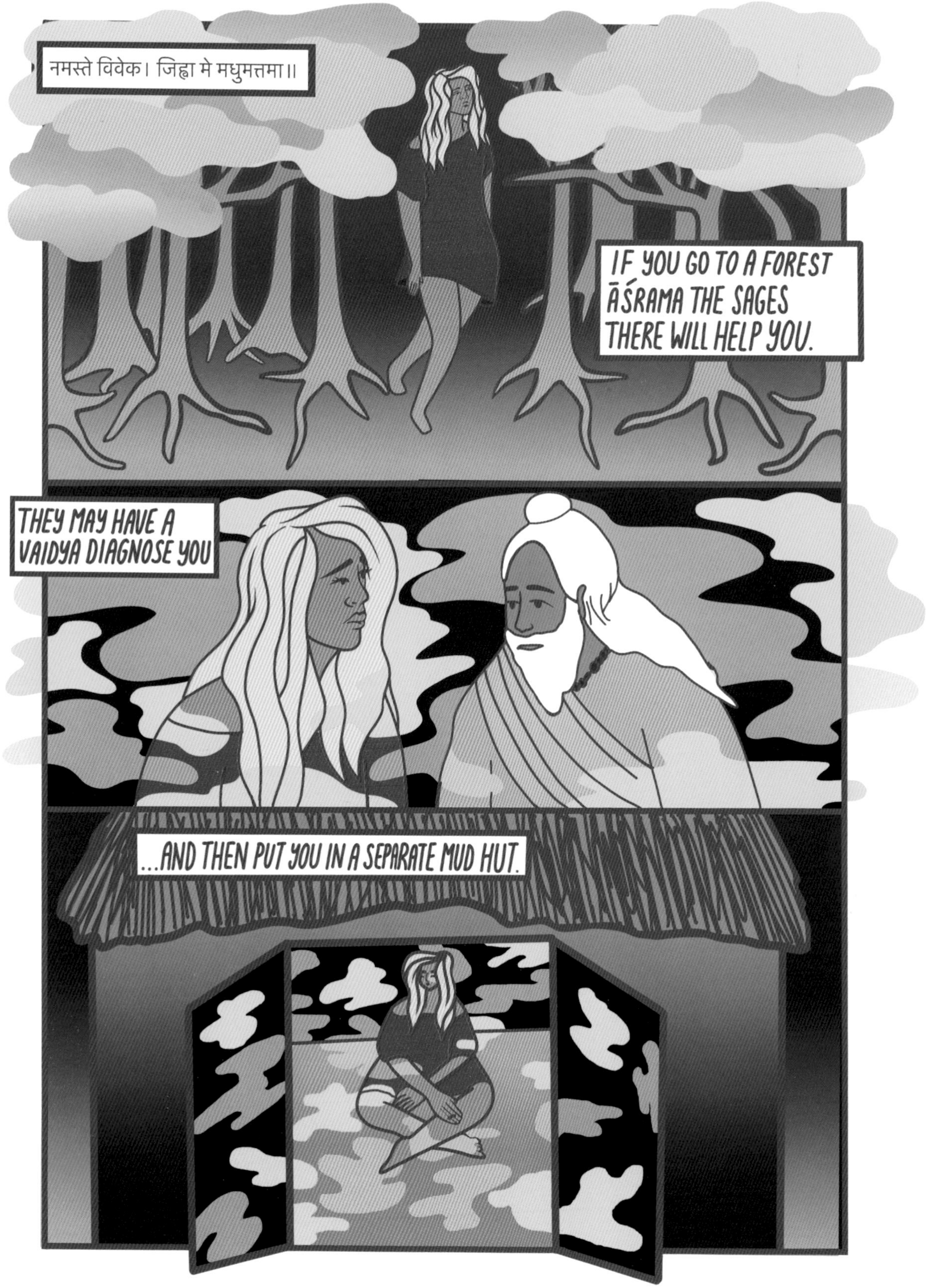
नमस्ते विवेक। जिह्वा मे मधुमत्तमा॥
IF YOU GO TO A FOREST ĀŚRAMA THE SAGES THERE WILL HELP YOU.
THEY MAY HAVE A VAIDYA DIAGNOSE YOU
...AND THEN PUT YOU IN A SEPARATE MUD HUT.

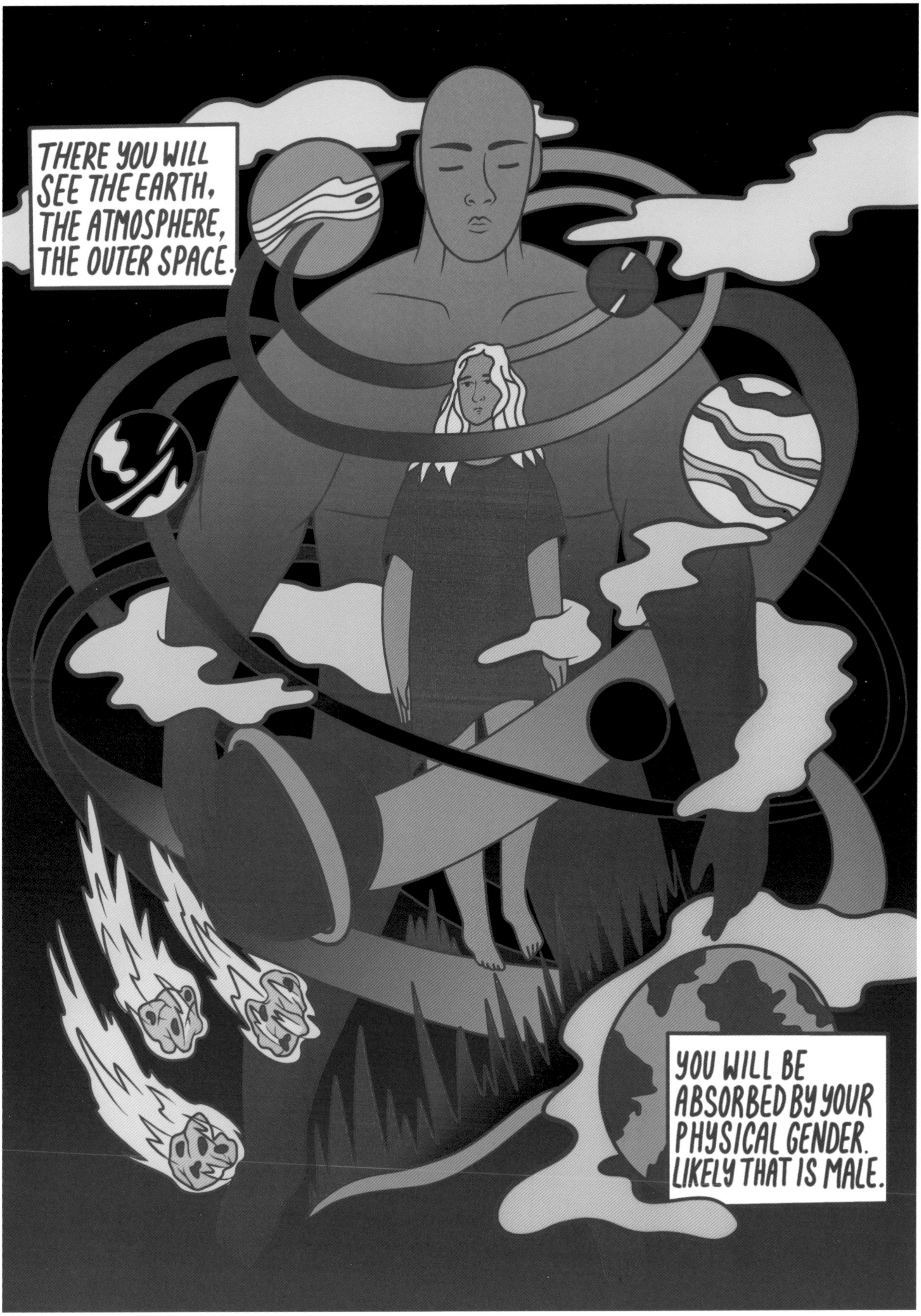
THERE YOU WILL SEE THE EARTH, THE ATMOSPHERE, THE OUTER SPACE.
YOU WILL BE ABSORBED BY YOUR PHYSICAL GENDER. LIKELY THAT IS MALE.

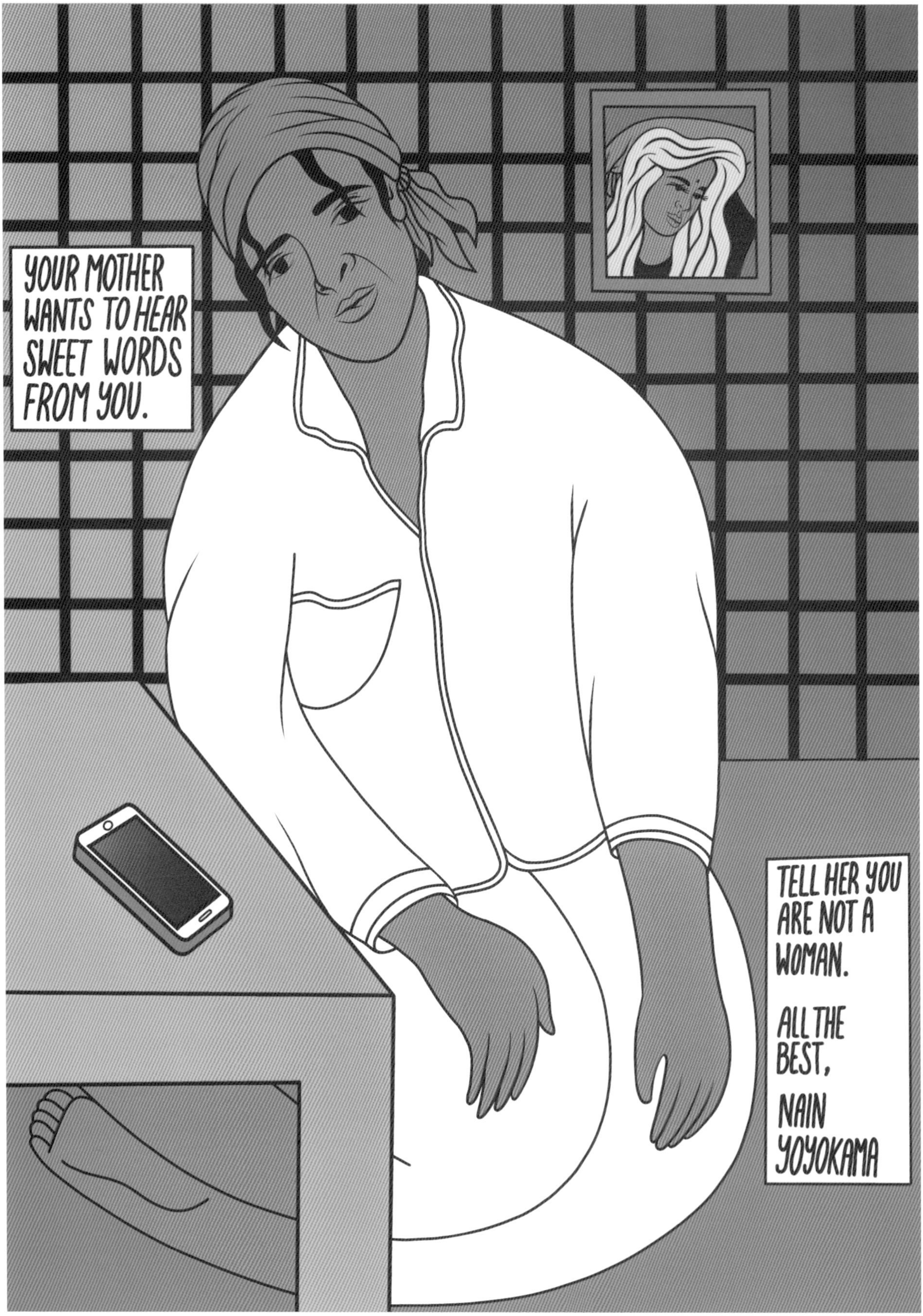
YOUR MOTHER WANTS TO HEAR SWEET WORDS FROM YOU.
TELL HER YOU ARE NOT A WOMAN.
ALL THE BEST,
NAIN YOYOKAMA

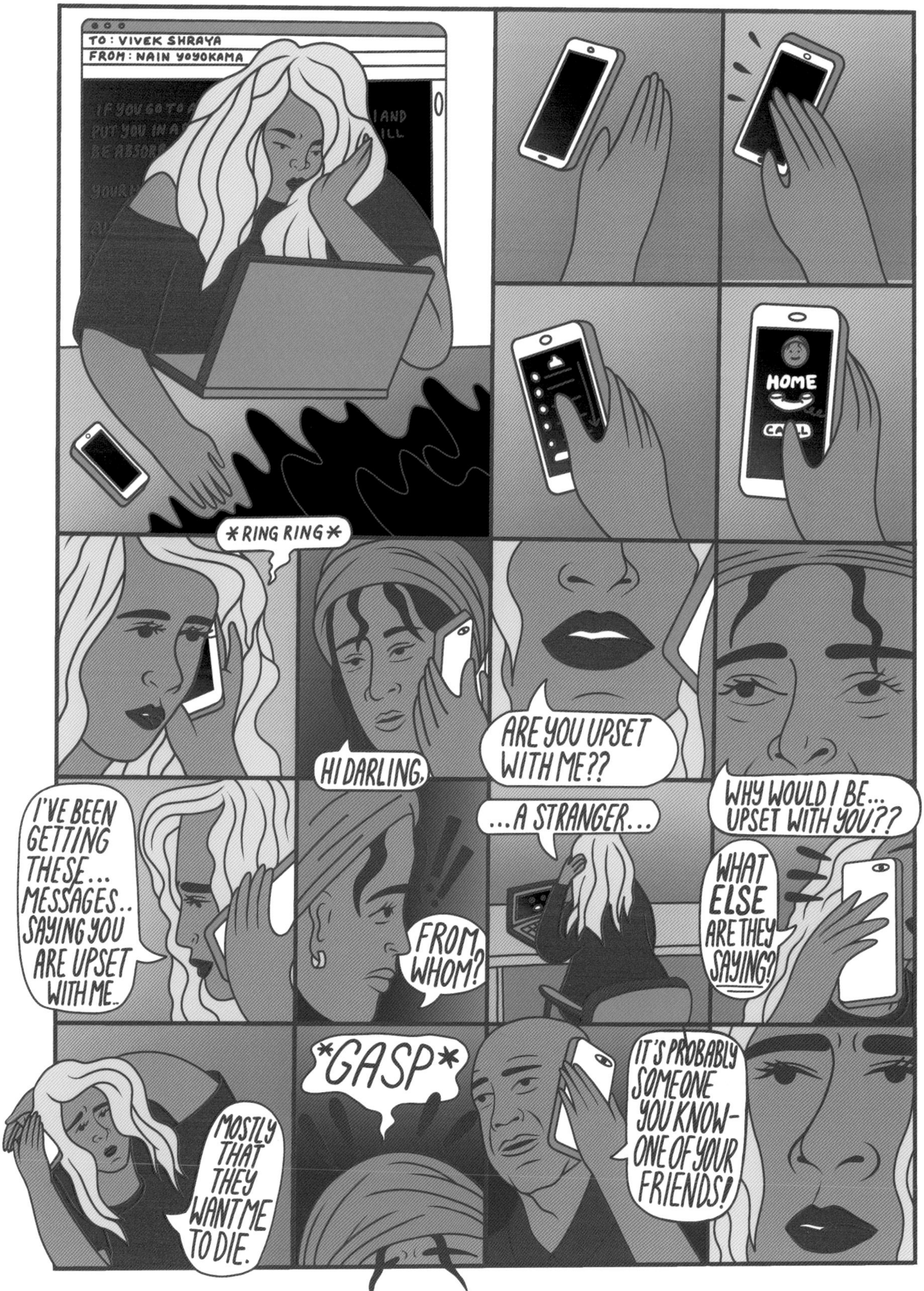
TO: VIVEK SHRAYA
FROM: NAIN YOYOKAMA
HOME
RING RING
HI DARLING.
ARE YOU UPSET WITH ME??
WHY WOULD I BE... UPSET WITH YOU??
I'VE BEEN GETTING THESE... MESSAGES.. SAYING YOU ARE UPSET WITH ME..
FROM WHOM?
...A STRANGER...
WHAT ELSE ARE THEY SAYING?
MOSTLY THAT THEY WANT ME TO DIE.
GASP
IT'S PROBABLY SOMEONE YOU KNOW- ONE OF YOUR FRIENDS!

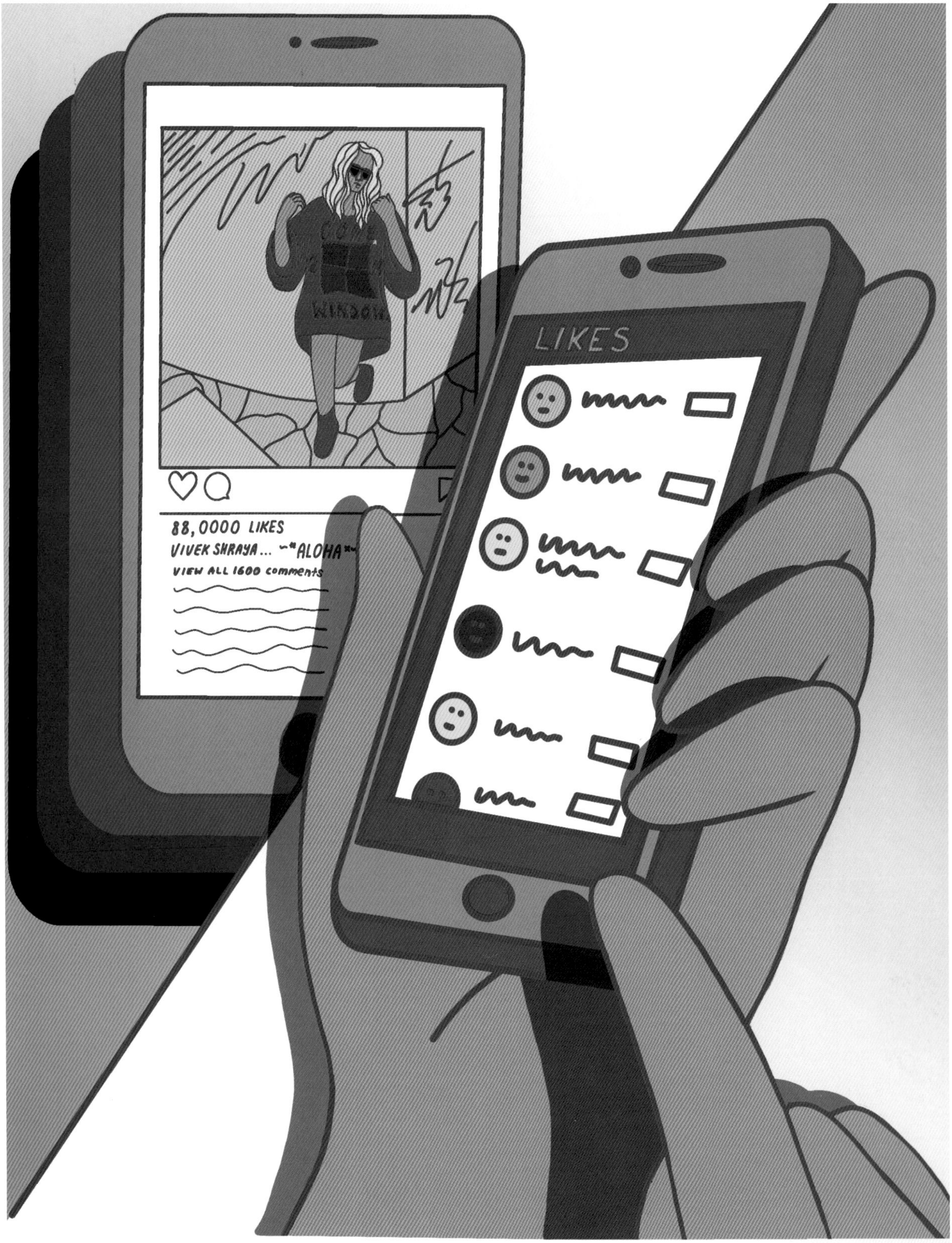
88,0000 LIKES
VIVEK SHRAYA ... ~*ALOHA*~
VIEW ALL 1600 comments
LIKES

I WONDERED IF I COULD DEDUCE WHO YOU WERE FROM MY FOLLOWERS.
MAYBE YOU WERE ONE OF THE PEOPLE WHO DIDN'T LIKE MY LAST SELFIE?

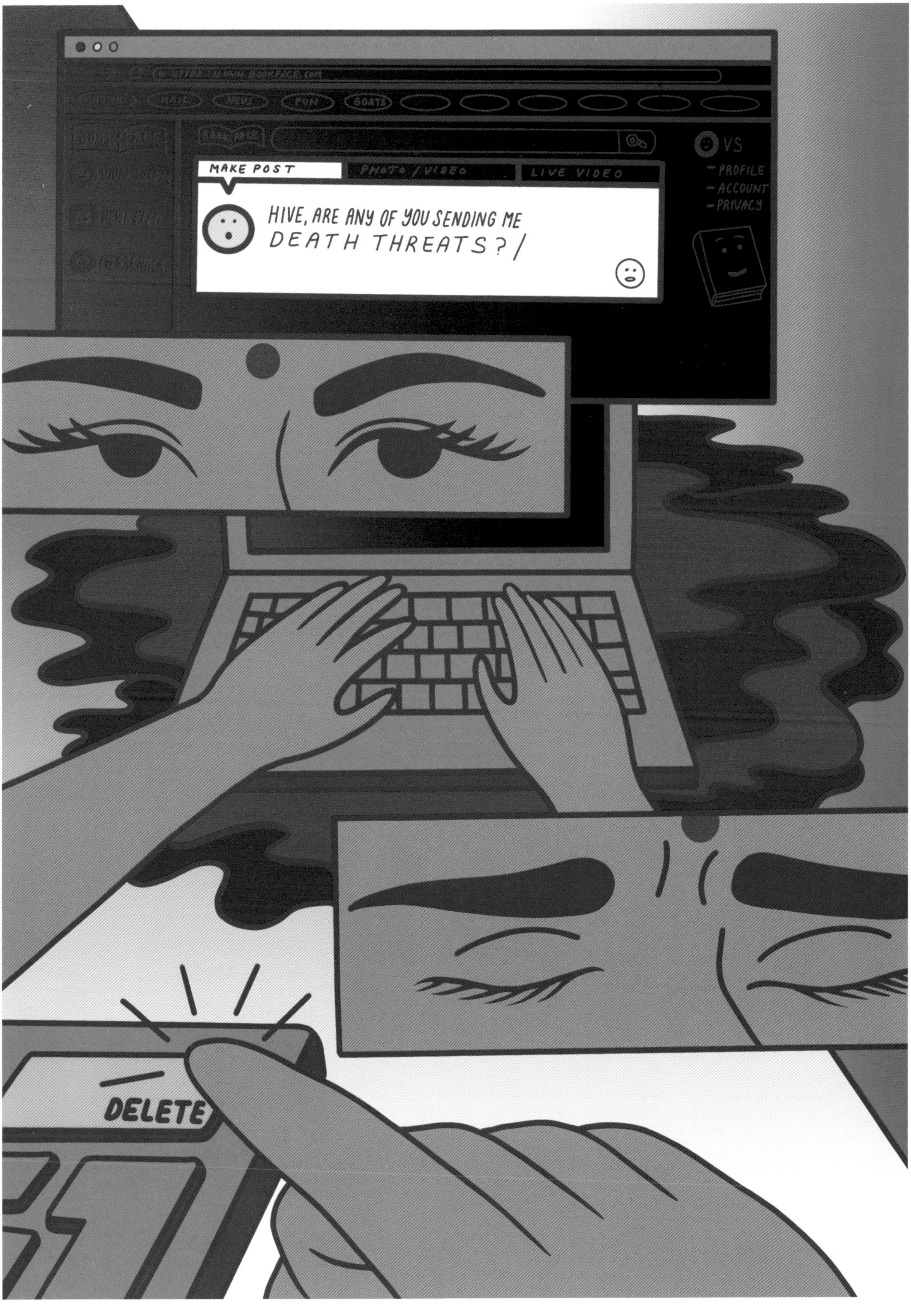
MAKE POST
PHOTO / VIDEO
LIVE VIDEO
HIVE, ARE ANY OF YOU SENDING ME
DEATH THREATS?
VS
PROFILE
ACCOUNT
PRIVACY
DELETE

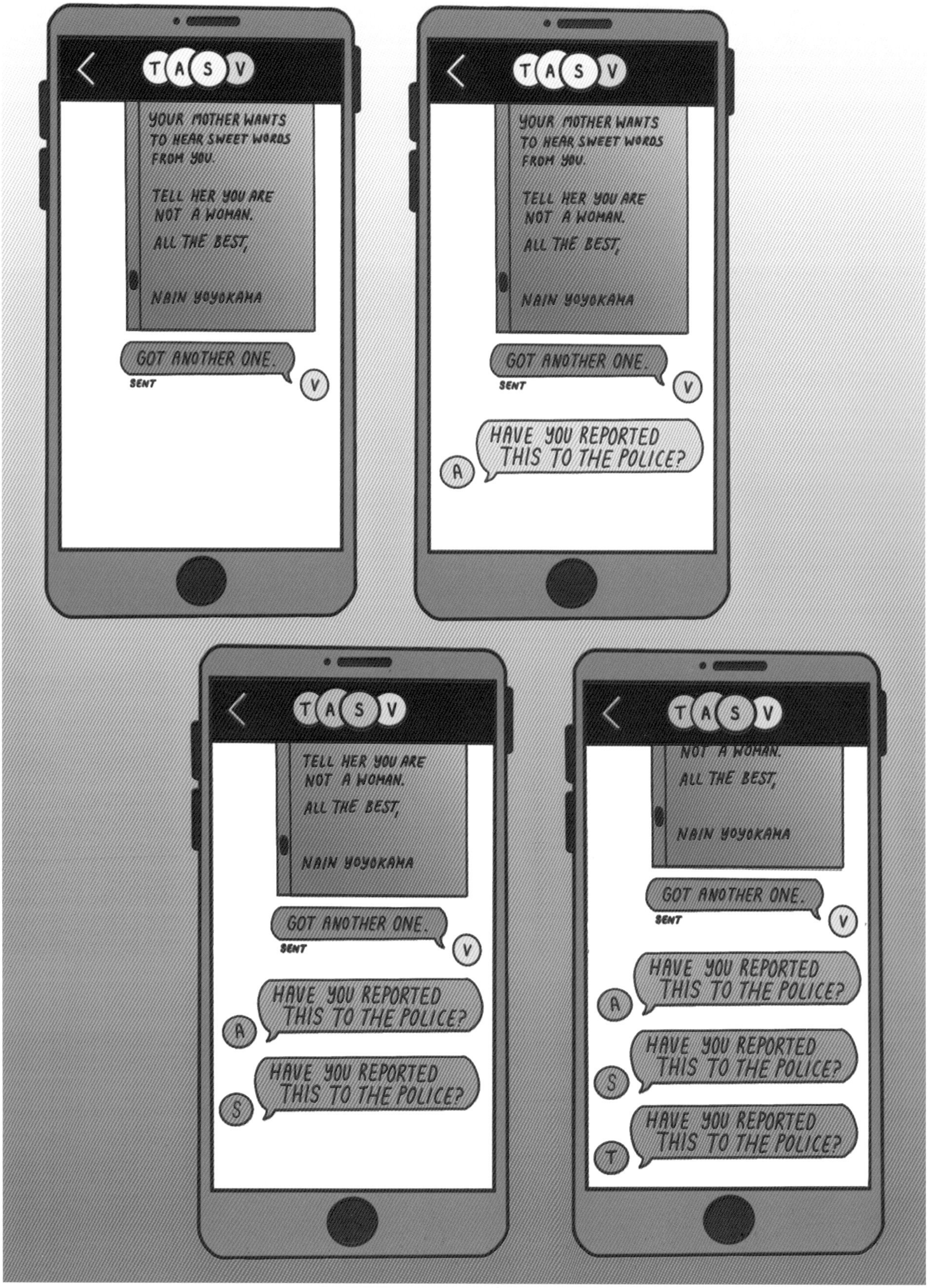
T A S V
YOUR MOTHER WANTS TO HEAR SWEET WORDS FROM YOU.
TELL HER YOU ARE NOT A WOMAN.
ALL THE BEST,
NAIN YOYOKAMA
GOT ANOTHER ONE.
SENT
V
T A S V
YOUR MOTHER WANTS TO HEAR SWEET WORDS FROM YOU.
TELL HER YOU ARE NOT A WOMAN.
ALL THE BEST,
NAIN YOYOKAMA
GOT ANOTHER ONE.
SENT
V
HAVE YOU REPORTED THIS TO THE POLICE?
A
T A S V
TELL HER YOU ARE NOT A WOMAN.
ALL THE BEST,
NAIN YOYOKAMA
GOT ANOTHER ONE.
SENT
V
HAVE YOU REPORTED THIS TO THE POLICE?
A
HAVE YOU REPORTED THIS TO THE POLICE?
S
T A S V
NOT A WOMAN.
ALL THE BEST,
NAIN YOYOKAMA
GOT ANOTHER ONE.
SENT
V
HAVE YOU REPORTED THIS TO THE POLICE?
A
HAVE YOU REPORTED THIS TO THE POLICE?
S
HAVE YOU REPORTED THIS TO THE POLICE?
T

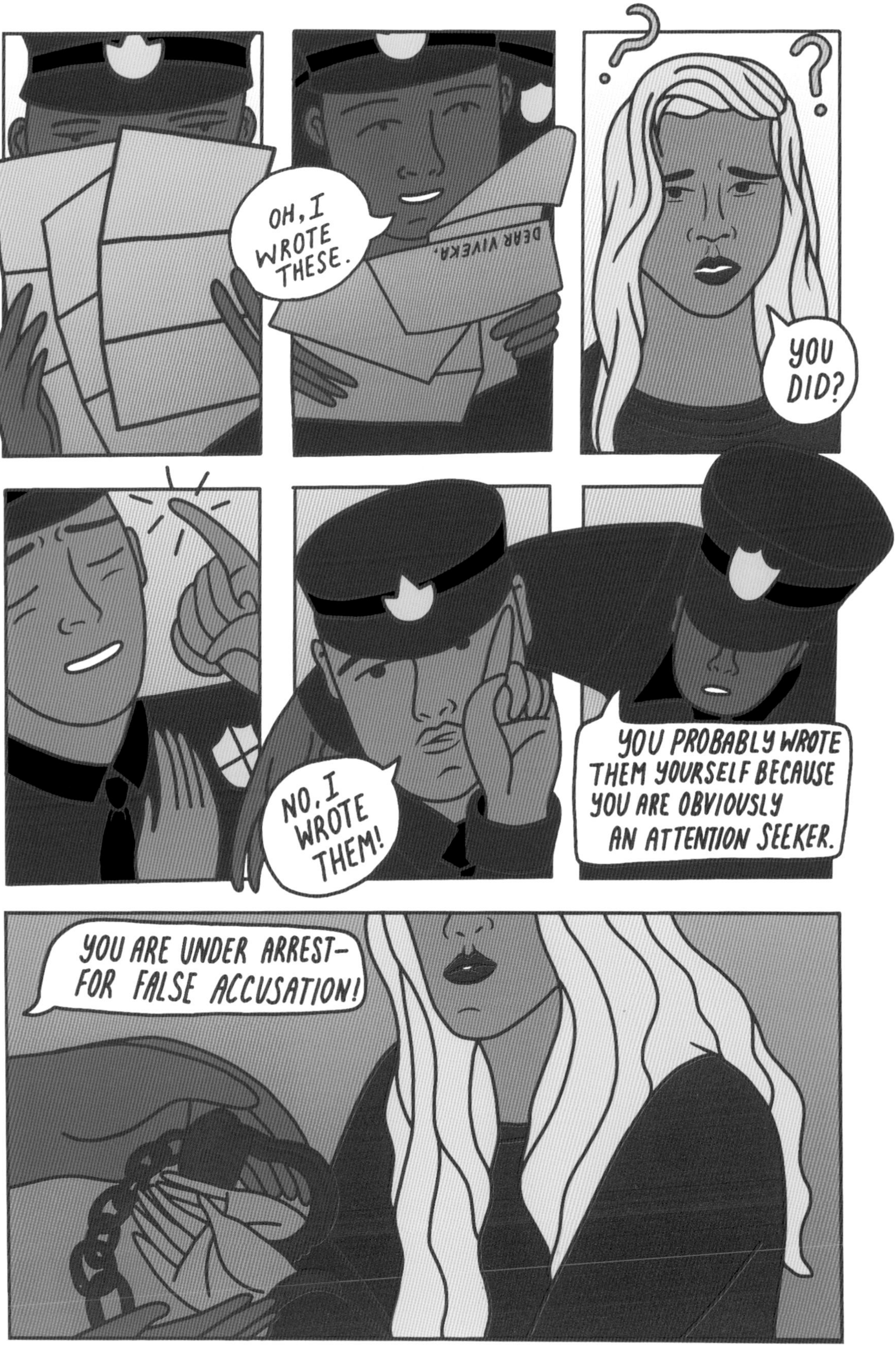

OH, I WROTE THESE.
DEAR VIVEKA,
YOU DID?
NO, I WROTE THEM!
YOU PROBABLY WROTE THEM YOURSELF BECAUSE YOU ARE OBVIOUSLY AN ATTENTION SEEKER.
YOU ARE UNDER ARREST- FOR FALSE ACCUSATION!

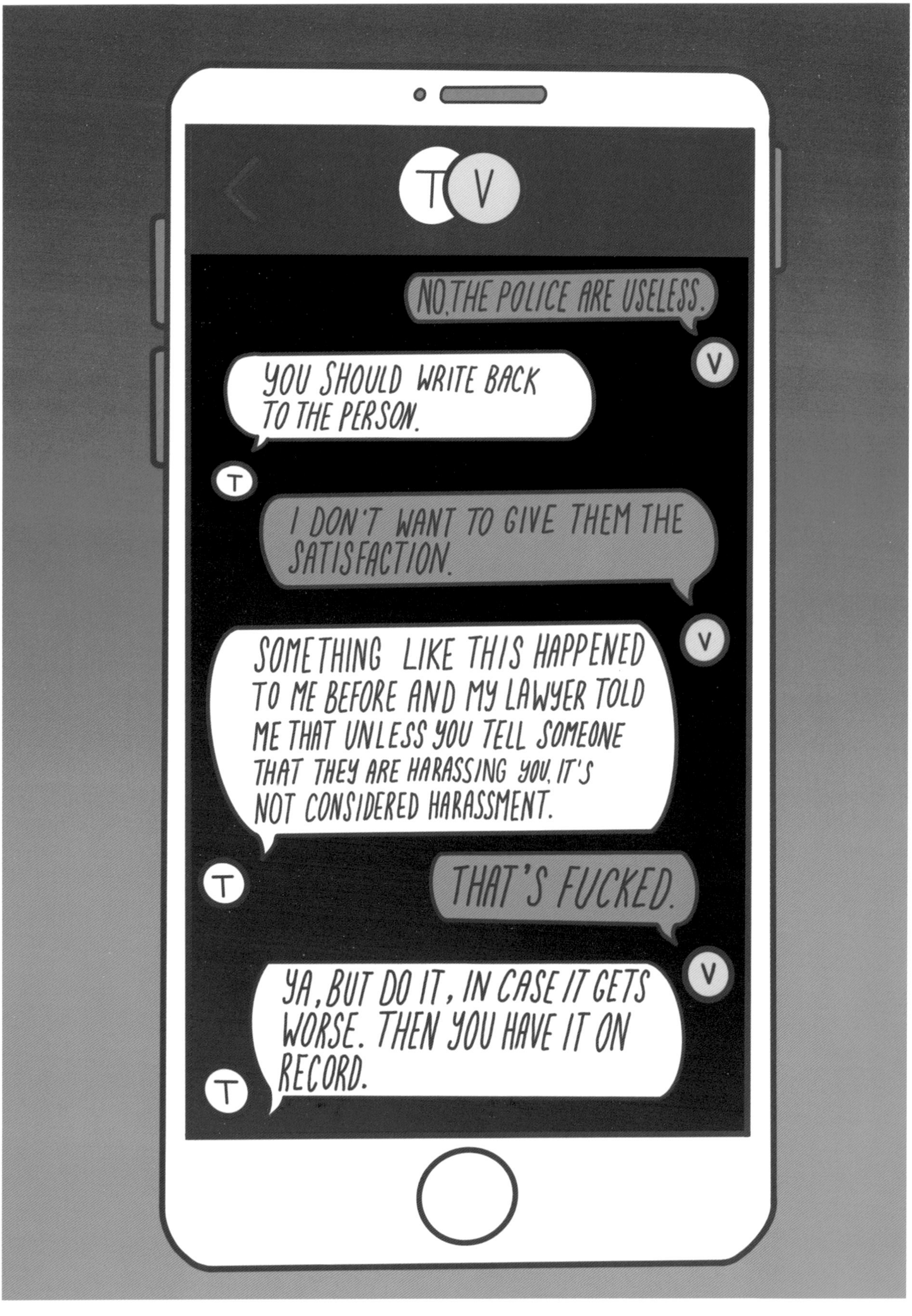

T
V
NO, THE POLICE ARE USELESS.
V
YOU SHOULD WRITE BACK TO THE PERSON.
T
I DON'T WANT TO GIVE THEM THE SATISFACTION.
V
SOMETHING LIKE THIS HAPPENED TO ME BEFORE AND MY LAWYER TOLD ME THAT UNLESS YOU TELL SOMEONE THAT THEY ARE HARASSING YOU, IT'S NOT CONSIDERED HARASSMENT.
T
THAT'S FUCKED.
V
YA, BUT DO IT, IN CASE IT GETS WORSE. THEN YOU HAVE IT ON RECORD.
T

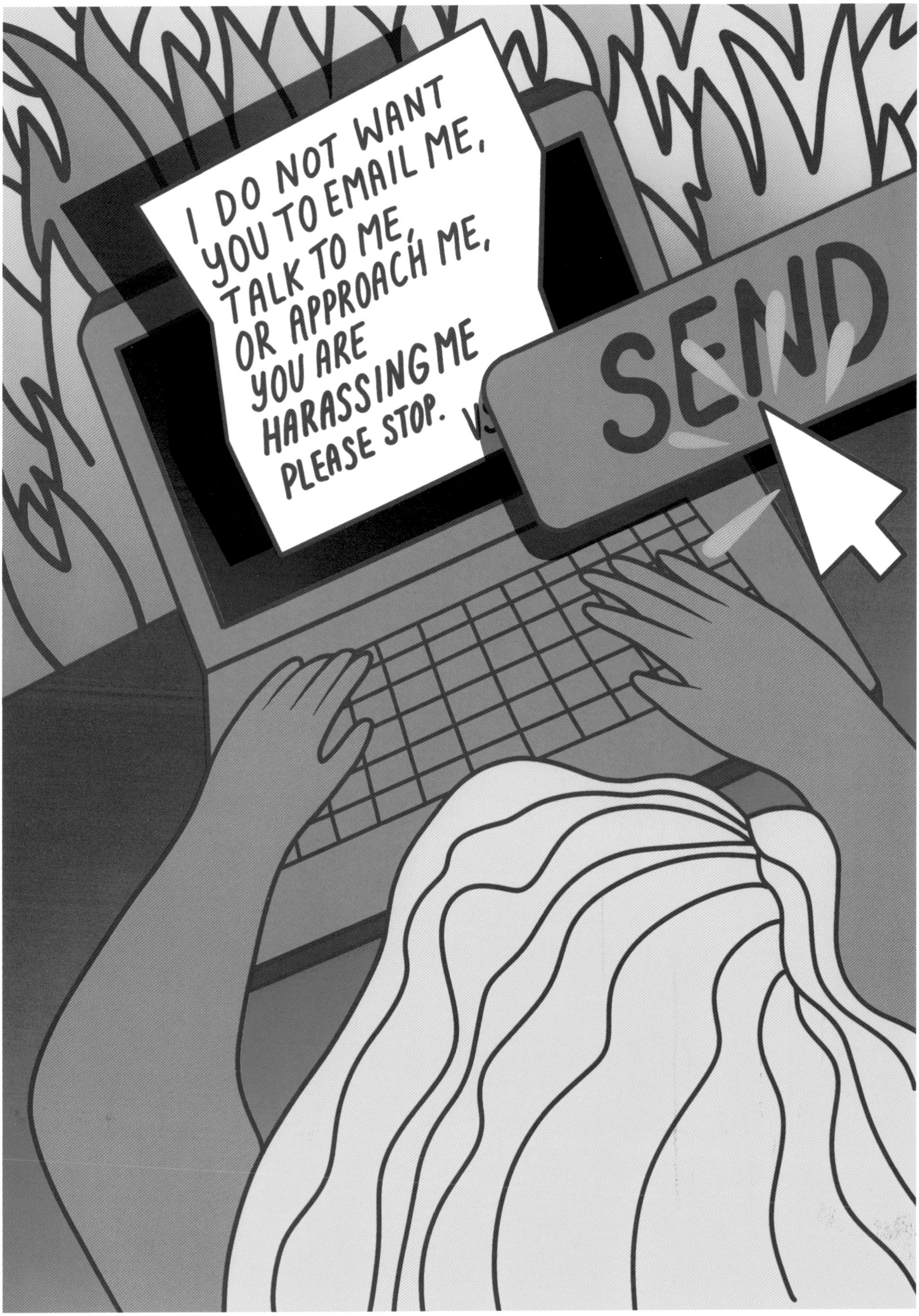
I DO NOT WANT YOU TO EMAIL ME, TALK TO ME, OR APPROACH ME, YOU ARE HARASSING ME PLEASE STOP.
SEND

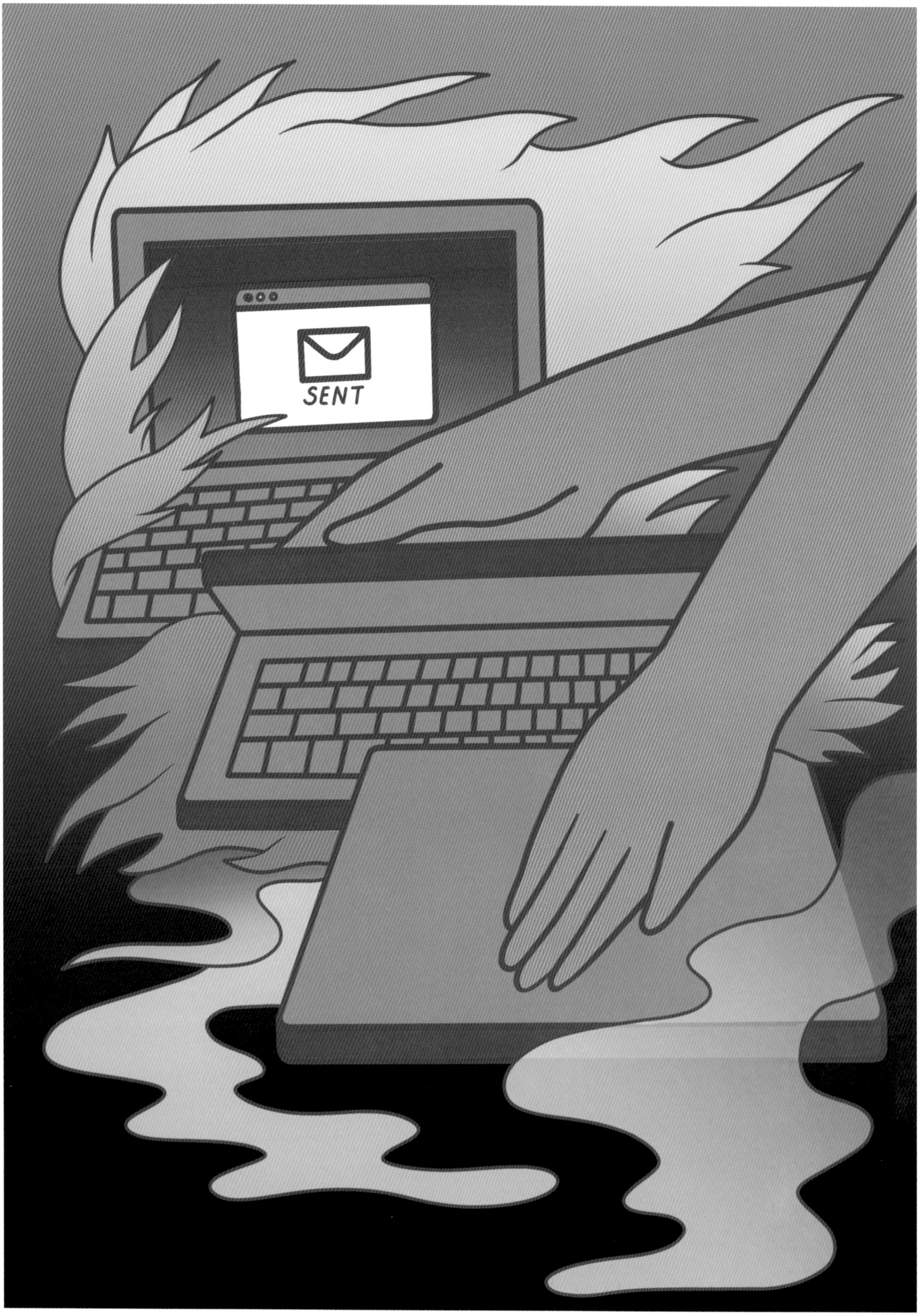
SENT

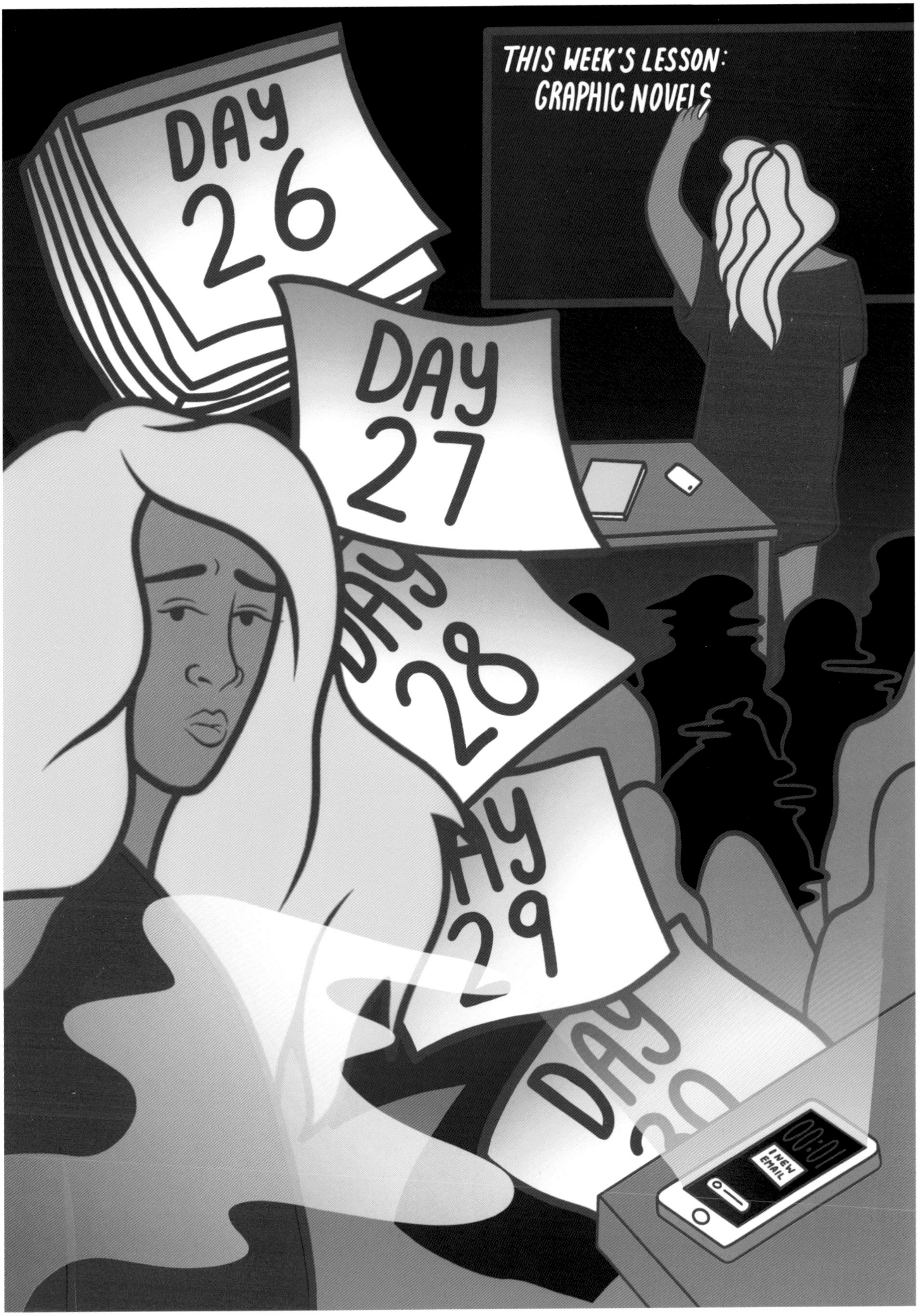
THIS WEEK'S LESSON:
GRAPHIC NOVELS
DAY 26
DAY 27
DAY 28
DAY 29
1 NEW EMAIL
00:01

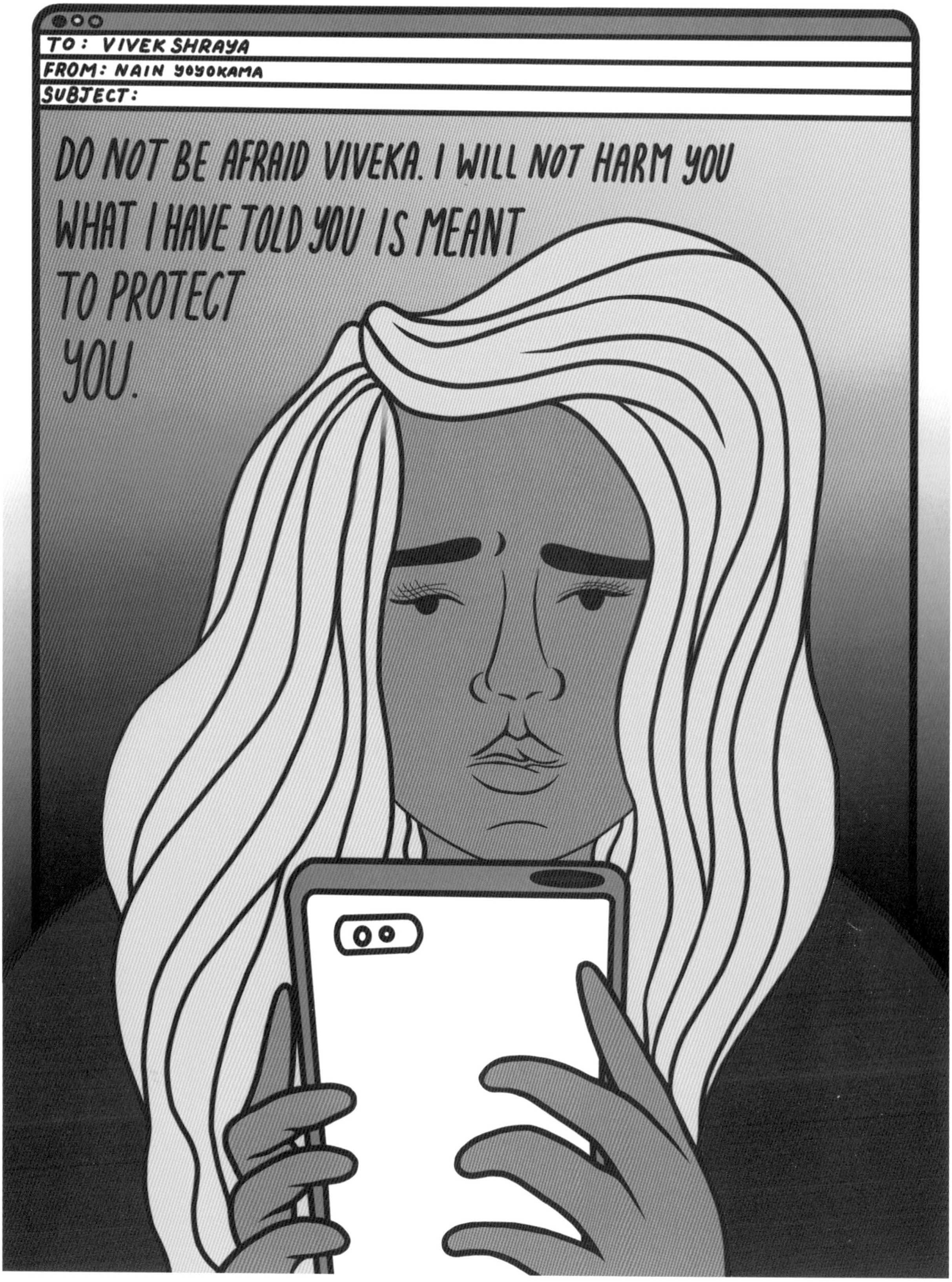
TO: VIVEK SHRAYA
FROM: NAIN YOYOKAMA
SUBJECT:
DO NOT BE AFRAID VIVEKA. I WILL NOT HARM YOU
WHAT I HAVE TOLD YOU IS MEANT TO PROTECT YOU.

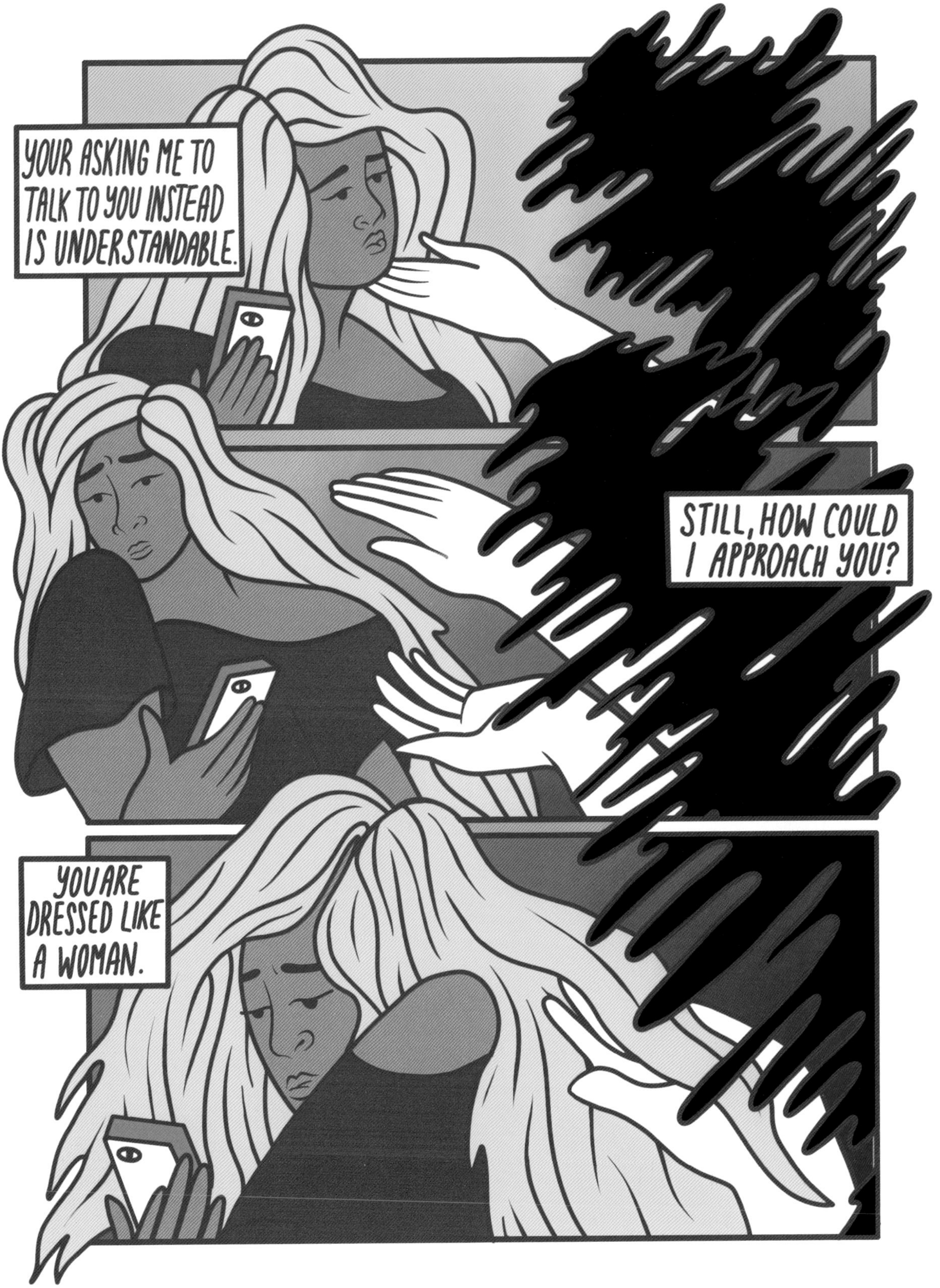
YOUR ASKING ME TO TALK TO YOU INSTEAD IS UNDERSTANDABLE.
STILL, HOW COULD I APPROACH YOU?
YOU ARE DRESSED LIKE A WOMAN.

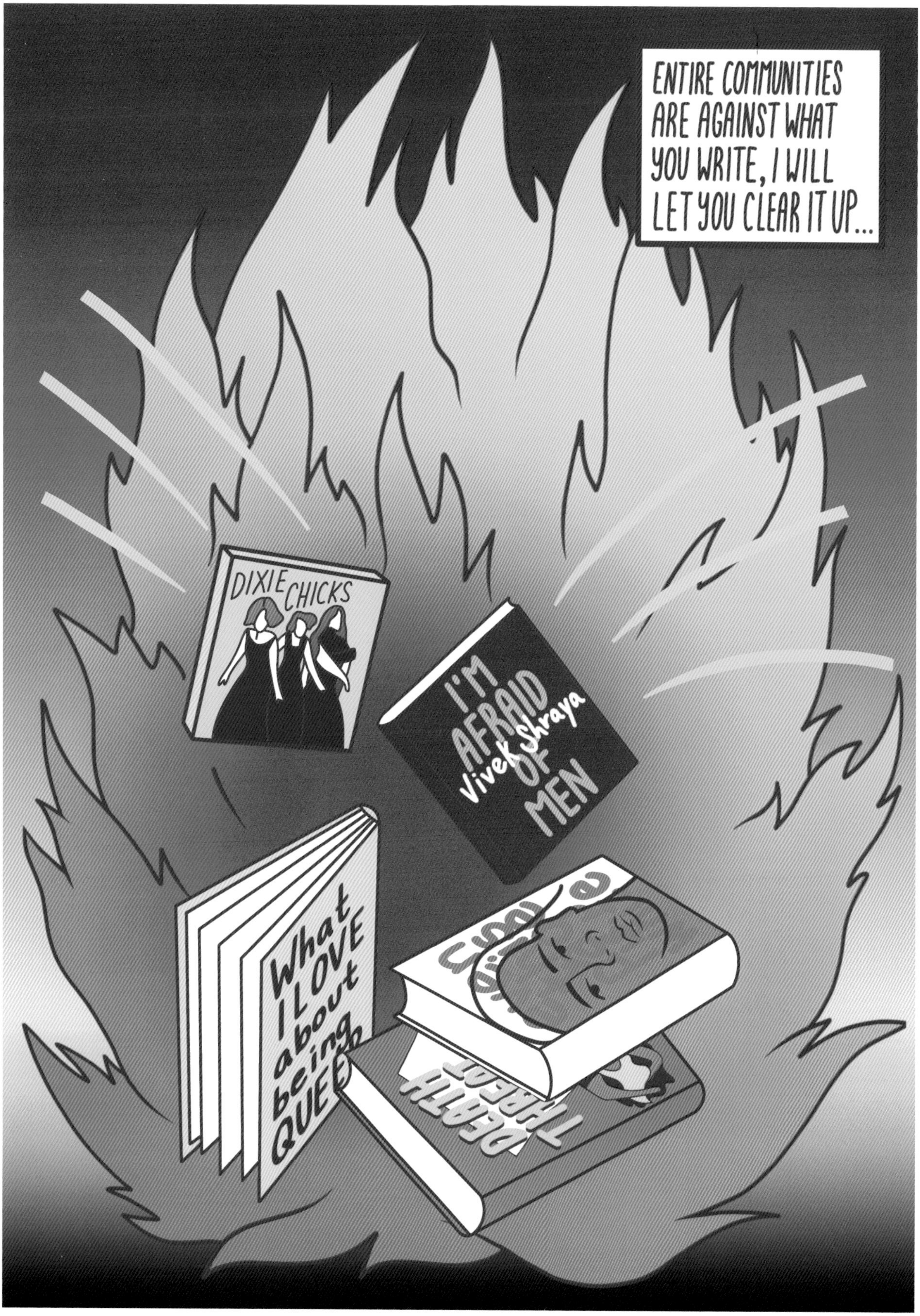
ENTIRE COMMUNITIES ARE AGAINST WHAT YOU WRITE, I WILL LET YOU CLEAR IT UP...
DIXIE CHICKS
I'M AFRAID OF MEN
Vivek Shraya
What I LOVE about being QUEE
DEATH THREAT

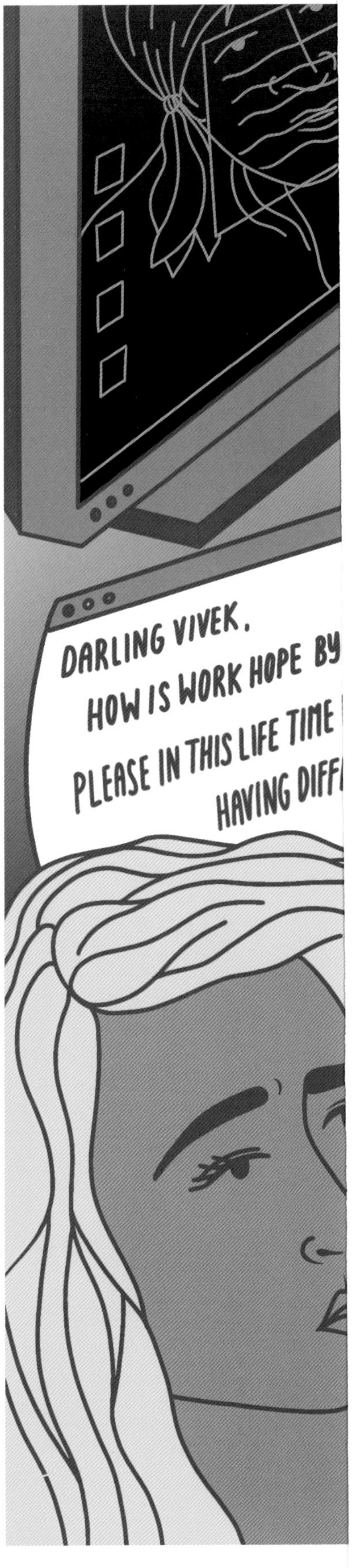
DARLING VIVEK,
HOW IS WORK HOPE BY
PLEASE IN THIS LIFE TIME
HAVING DIFF

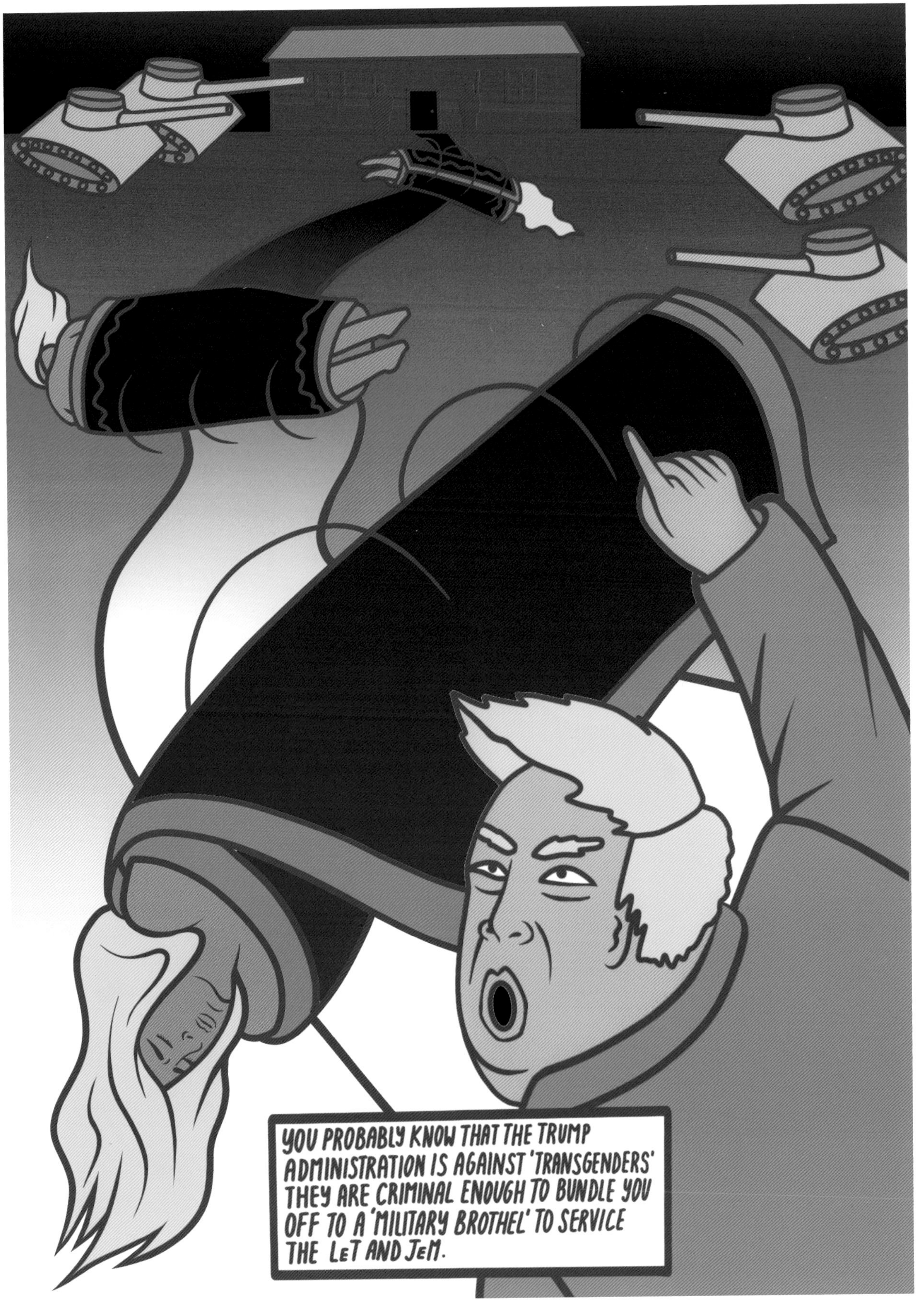
YOU PROBABLY KNOW THAT THE TRUMP ADMINISTRATION IS AGAINST 'TRANSGENDERS' THEY ARE CRIMINAL ENOUGH TO BUNDLE YOU OFF TO A 'MILITARY BROTHEL' TO SERVICE THE LeT AND JeM.

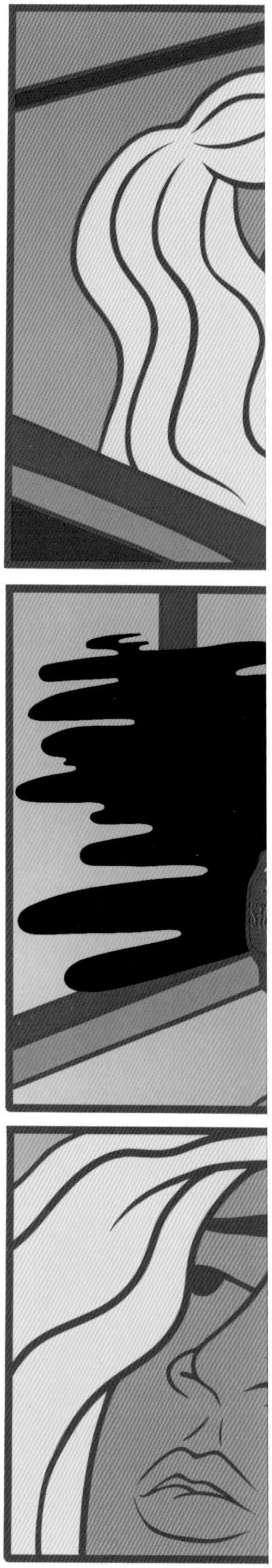

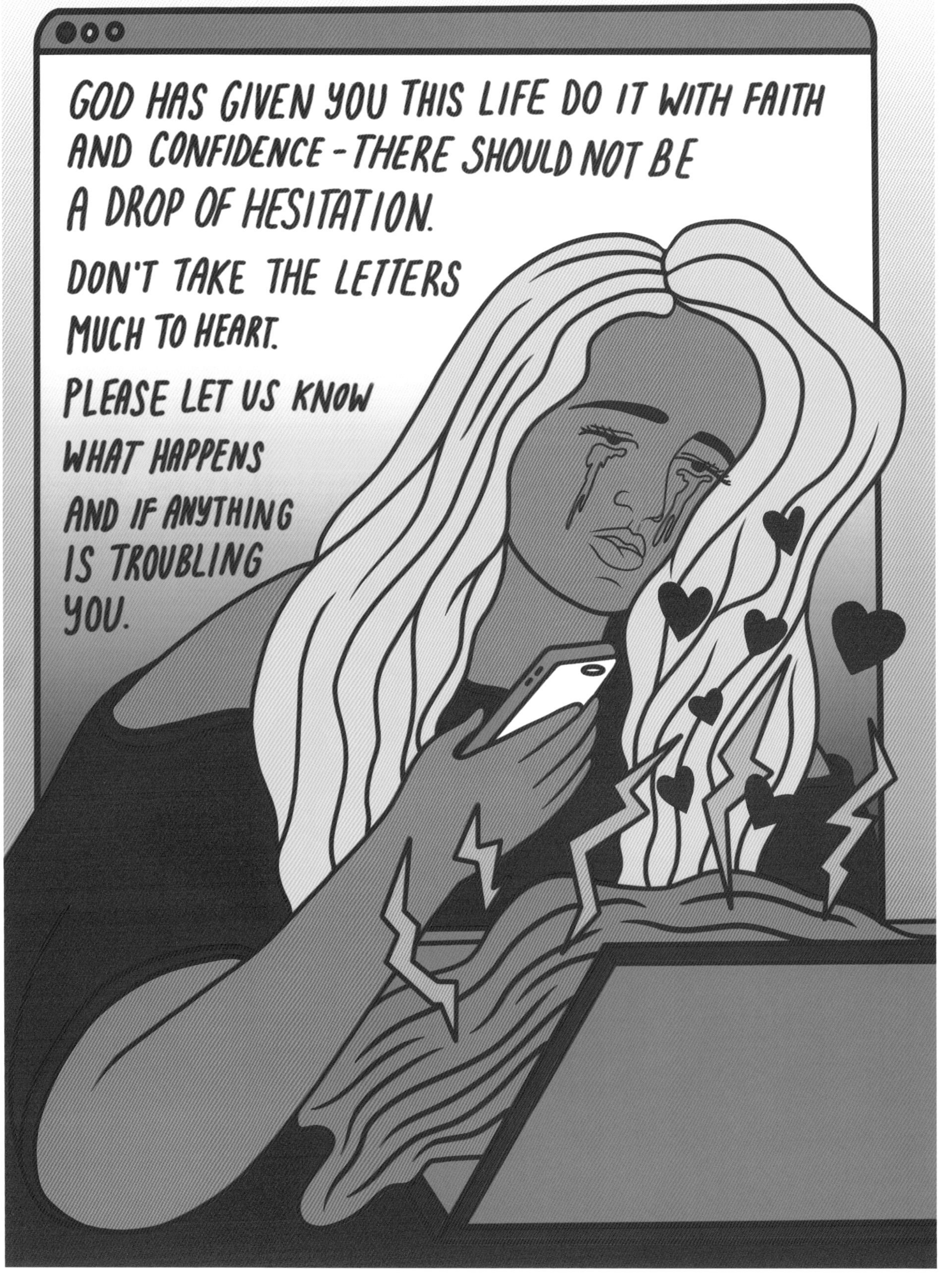
GOD HAS GIVEN YOU THIS LIFE DO IT WITH FAITH AND CONFIDENCE - THERE SHOULD NOT BE A DROP OF HESITATION.
DON'T TAKE THE LETTERS MUCH TO HEART.
PLEASE LET US KNOW WHAT HAPPENS AND IF ANYTHING IS TROUBLING YOU.

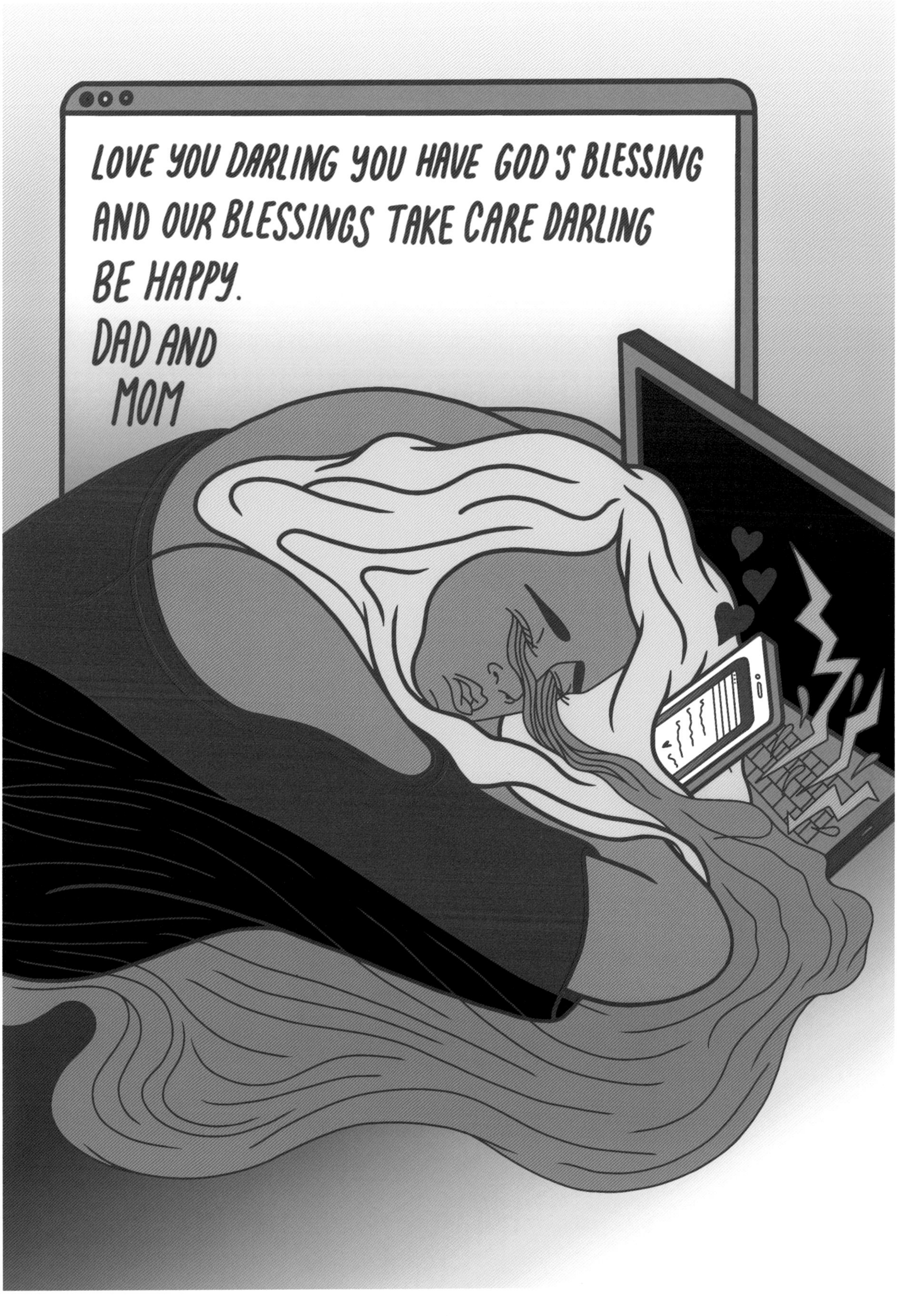
LOVE YOU DARLING YOU HAVE GOD'S BLESSING
AND OUR BLESSINGS TAKE CARE DARLING
BE HAPPY.
DAD AND
MOM

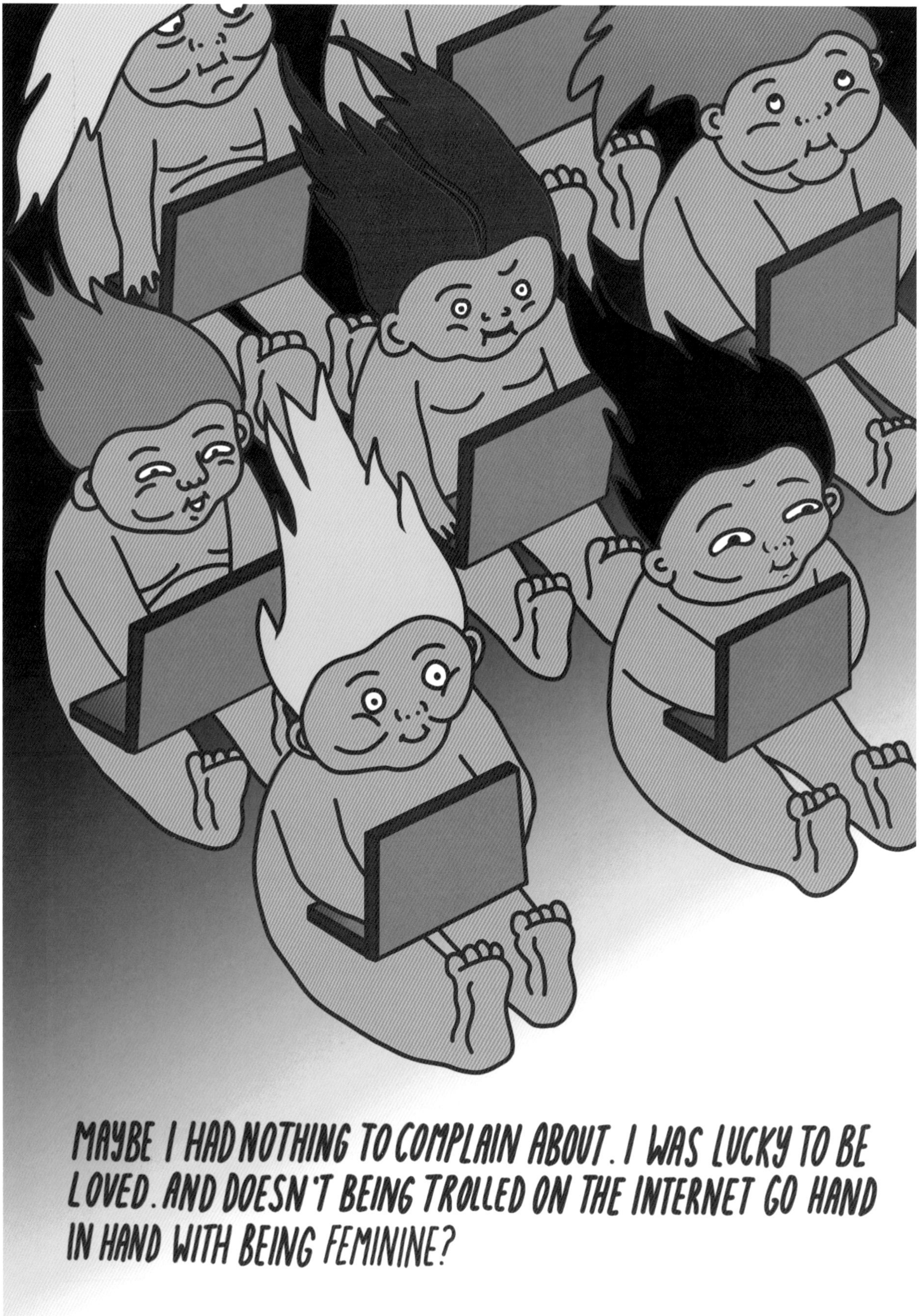
MAYBE I HAD NOTHING TO COMPLAIN ABOUT. I WAS LUCKY TO BE LOVED. AND DOESN'T BEING TROLLED ON THE INTERNET GO HAND IN HAND WITH BEING FEMININE?

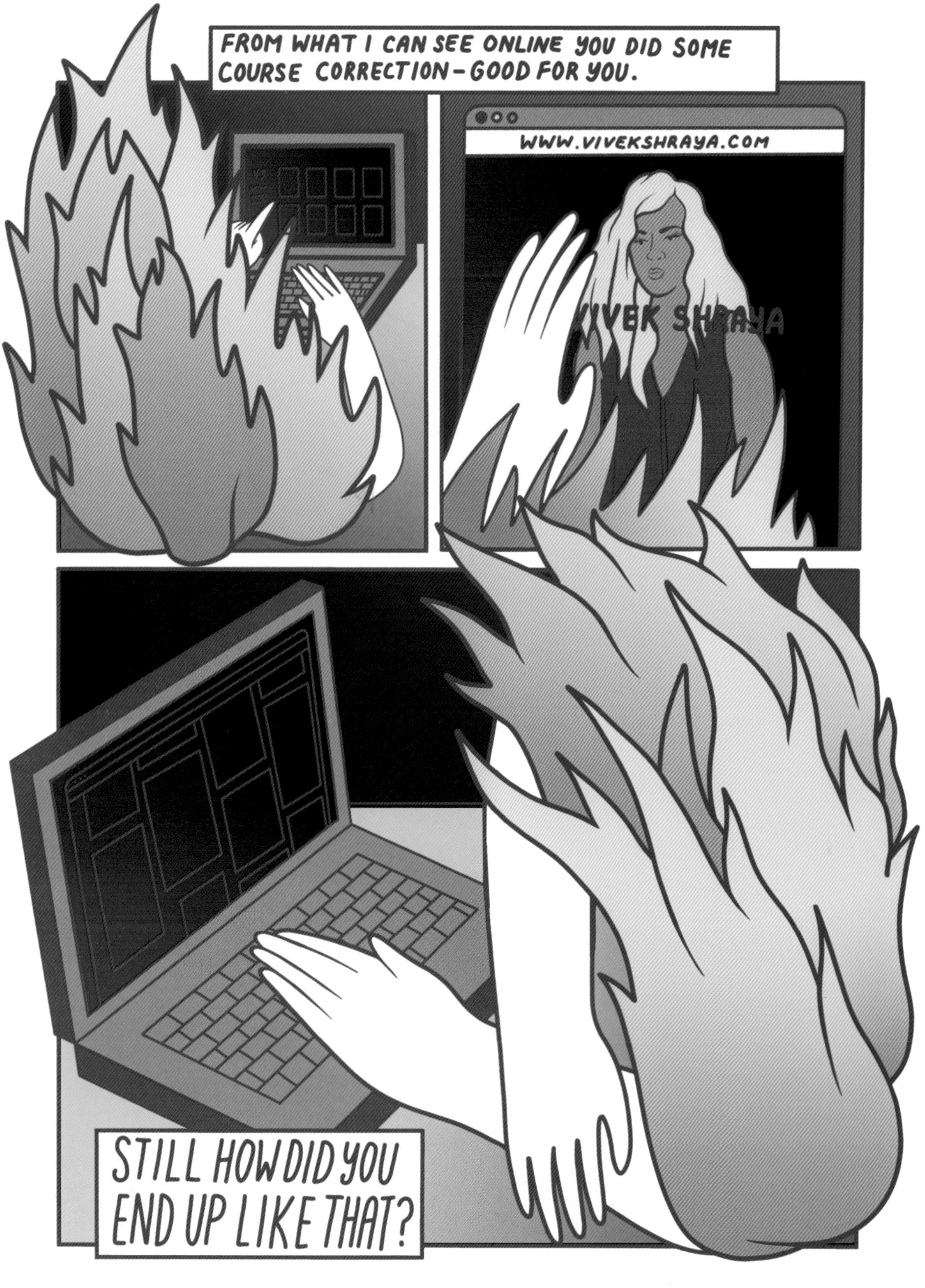
FROM WHAT I CAN SEE ONLINE YOU DID SOME COURSE CORRECTION - GOOD FOR YOU.
WWW.VIVEKSHRAYA.COM
STILL HOW DID YOU END UP LIKE THAT?

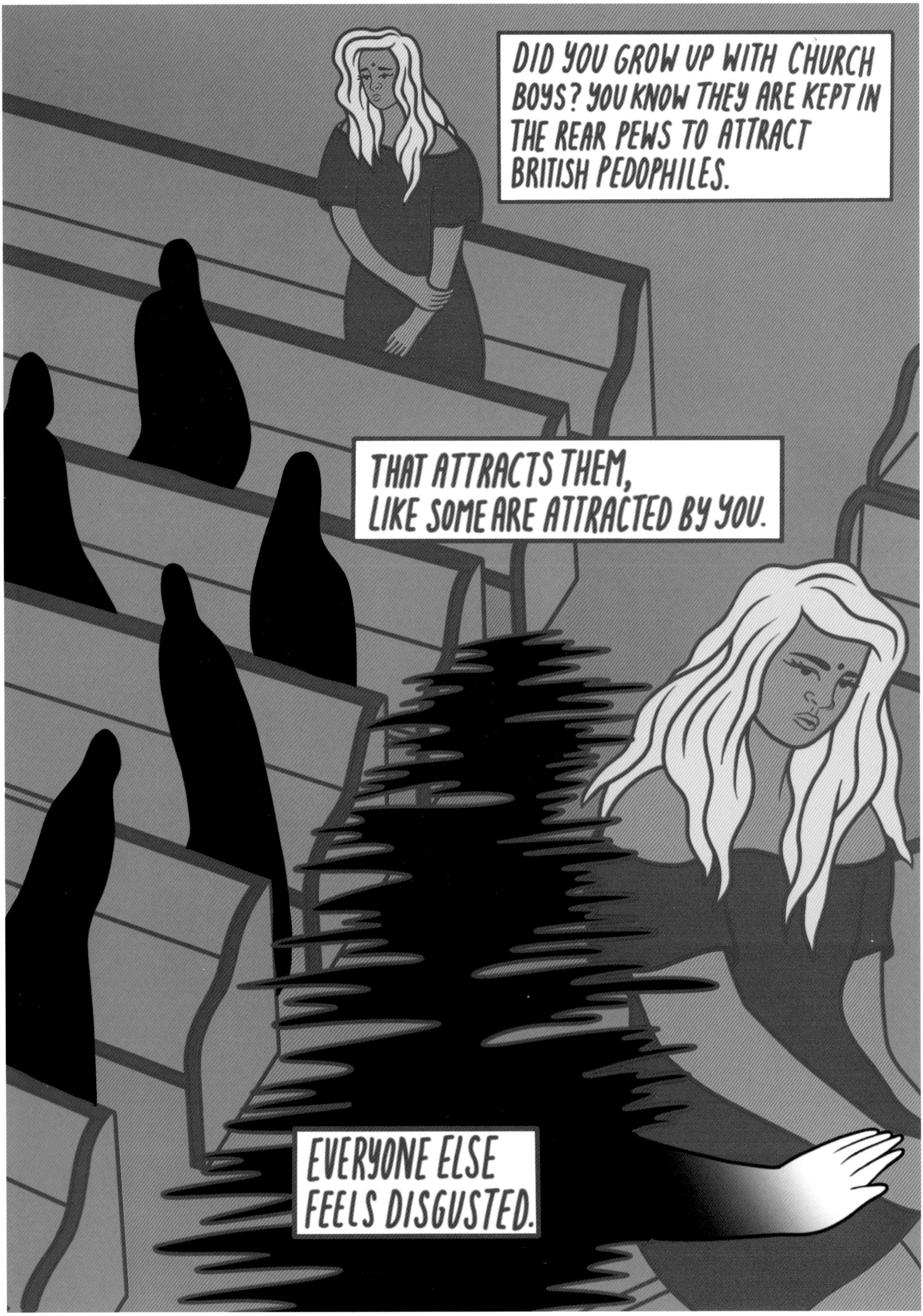
DID YOU GROW UP WITH CHURCH BOYS? YOU KNOW THEY ARE KEPT IN THE REAR PEWS TO ATTRACT BRITISH PEDOPHILES.
THAT ATTRACTS THEM, LIKE SOME ARE ATTRACTED BY YOU.
EVERYONE ELSE FEELS DISGUSTED.

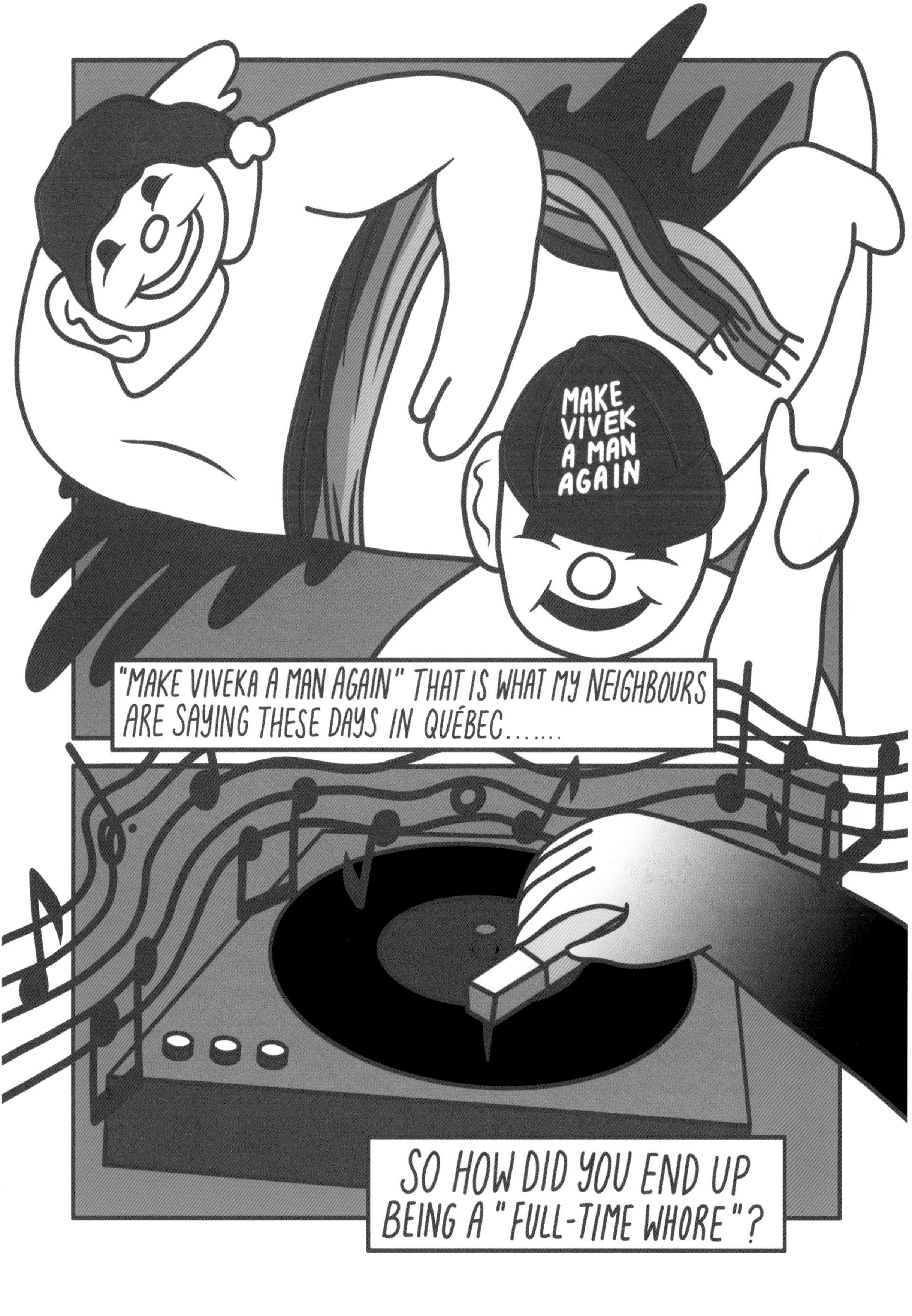

MAKE VIVEK A MAN AGAIN
"MAKE VIVEKA A MAN AGAIN" THAT IS WHAT MY NEIGHBOURS ARE SAYING THESE DAYS IN QUÉBEC.......
SO HOW DID YOU END UP BEING A "FULL-TIME WHORE"?

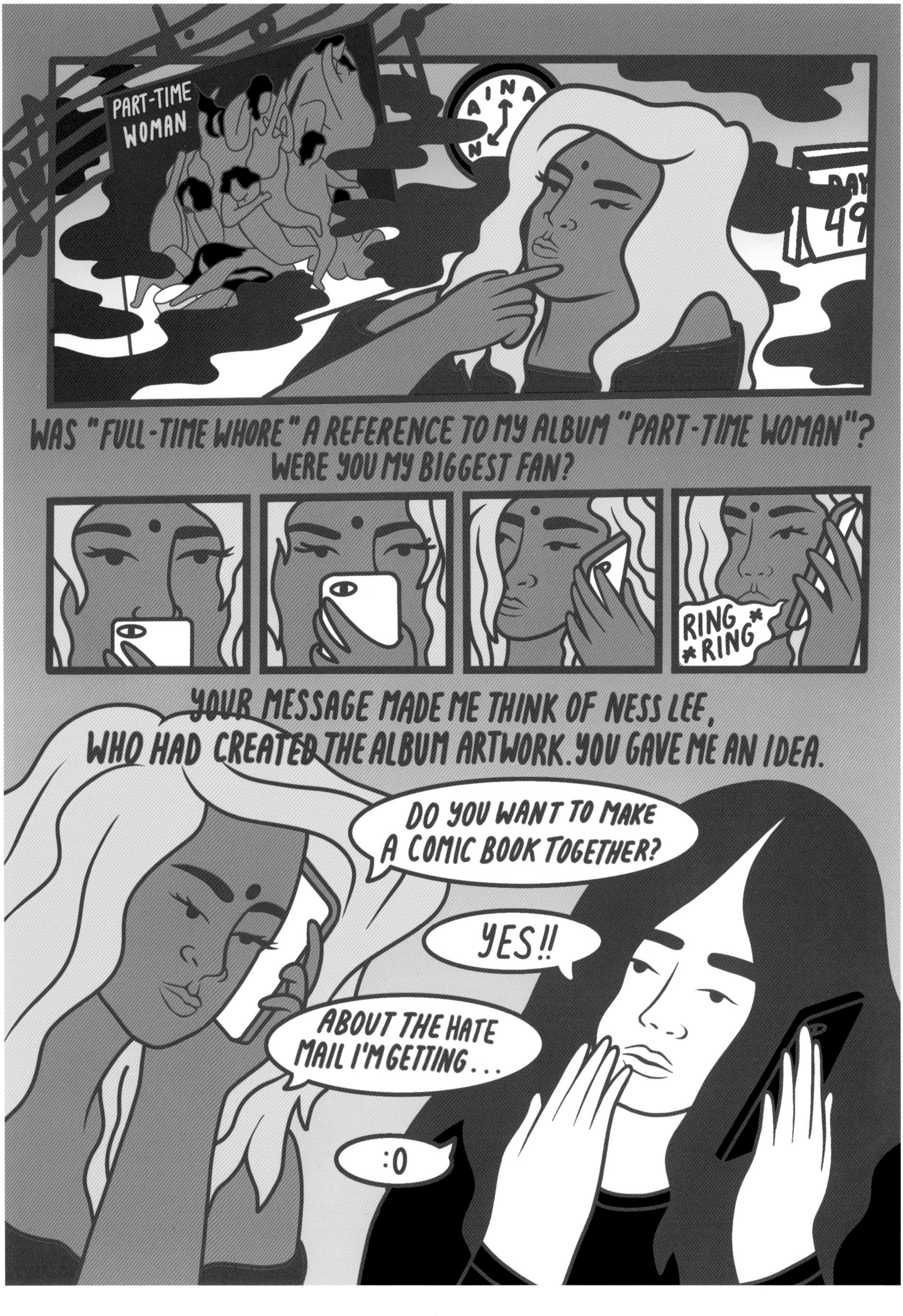
PART-TIME WOMAN
DAY 49
WAS "FULL-TIME WHORE" A REFERENCE TO MY ALBUM "PART-TIME WOMAN"? WERE YOU MY BIGGEST FAN?
RING* *RING
YOUR MESSAGE MADE ME THINK OF NESS LEE, WHO HAD CREATED THE ALBUM ARTWORK. YOU GAVE ME AN IDEA.
DO YOU WANT TO MAKE A COMIC BOOK TOGETHER?
YES!!
ABOUT THE HATE MAIL I'M GETTING...
:0

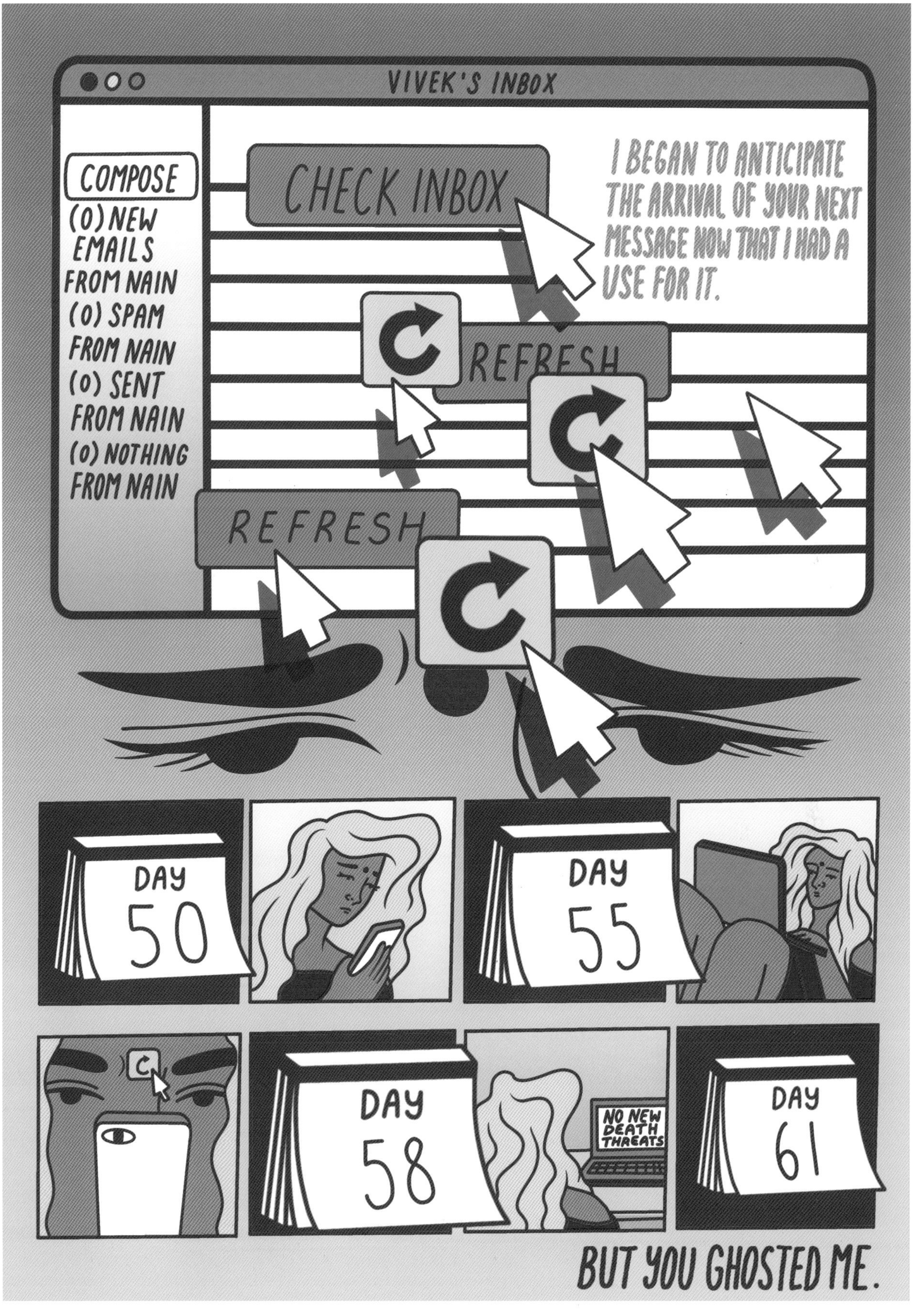
VIVEK'S INBOX
COMPOSE
(0) NEW EMAILS FROM NAIN
(0) SPAM FROM NAIN
(0) SENT FROM NAIN
(0) NOTHING FROM NAIN
CHECK INBOX
I BEGAN TO ANTICIPATE THE ARRIVAL OF YOUR NEXT MESSAGE NOW THAT I HAD A USE FOR IT.
REFRESH
REFRESH
DAY 50
DAY 55
DAY 58
NO NEW DEATH THREATS
DAY 61
BUT YOU GHOSTED ME.

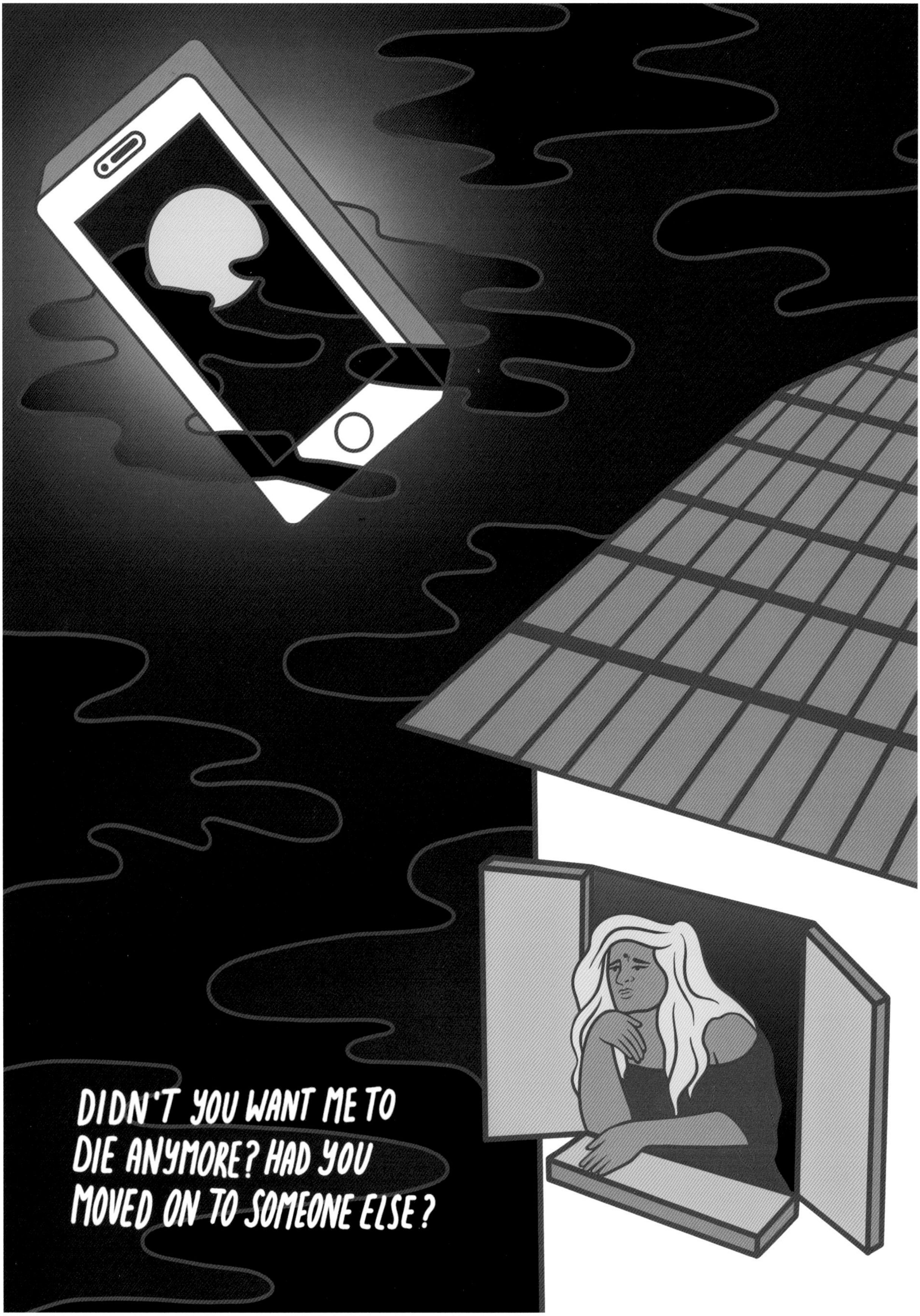
DIDN'T YOU WANT ME TO
DIE ANYMORE? HAD YOU
MOVED ON TO SOMEONE ELSE?

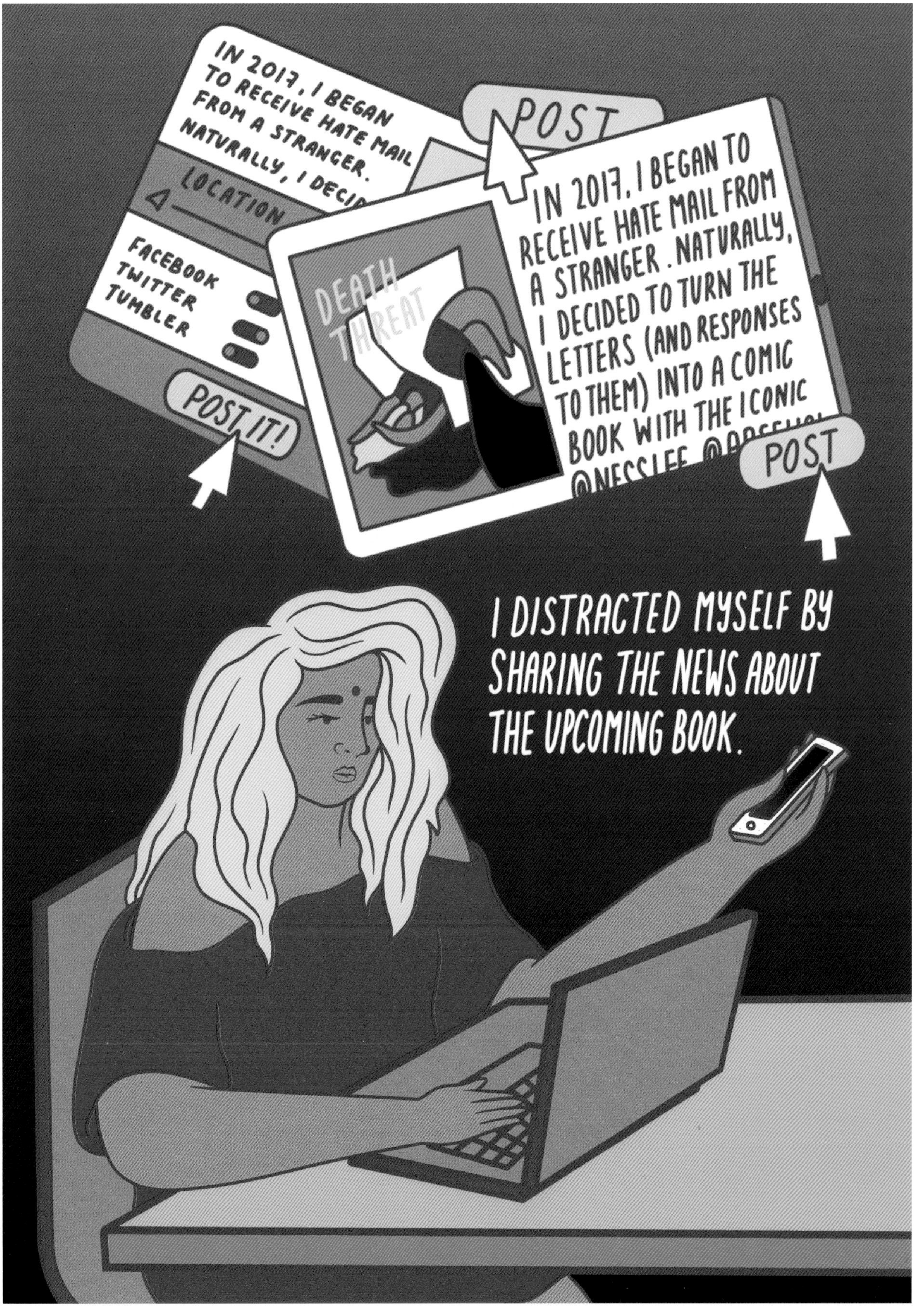
IN 2017, I BEGAN TO RECEIVE HATE MAIL FROM A STRANGER. NATURALLY, I
LOCATION
FACEBOOK
TWITTER
TUMBLER
POST IT!
POST
DEATH THREAT
IN 2017, I BEGAN TO RECEIVE HATE MAIL FROM A STRANGER. NATURALLY, I DECIDED TO TURN THE LETTERS (AND RESPONSES TO THEM) INTO A COMIC BOOK WITH THE ICONIC
POST
I DISTRACTED MYSELF BY SHARING THE NEWS ABOUT THE UPCOMING BOOK.

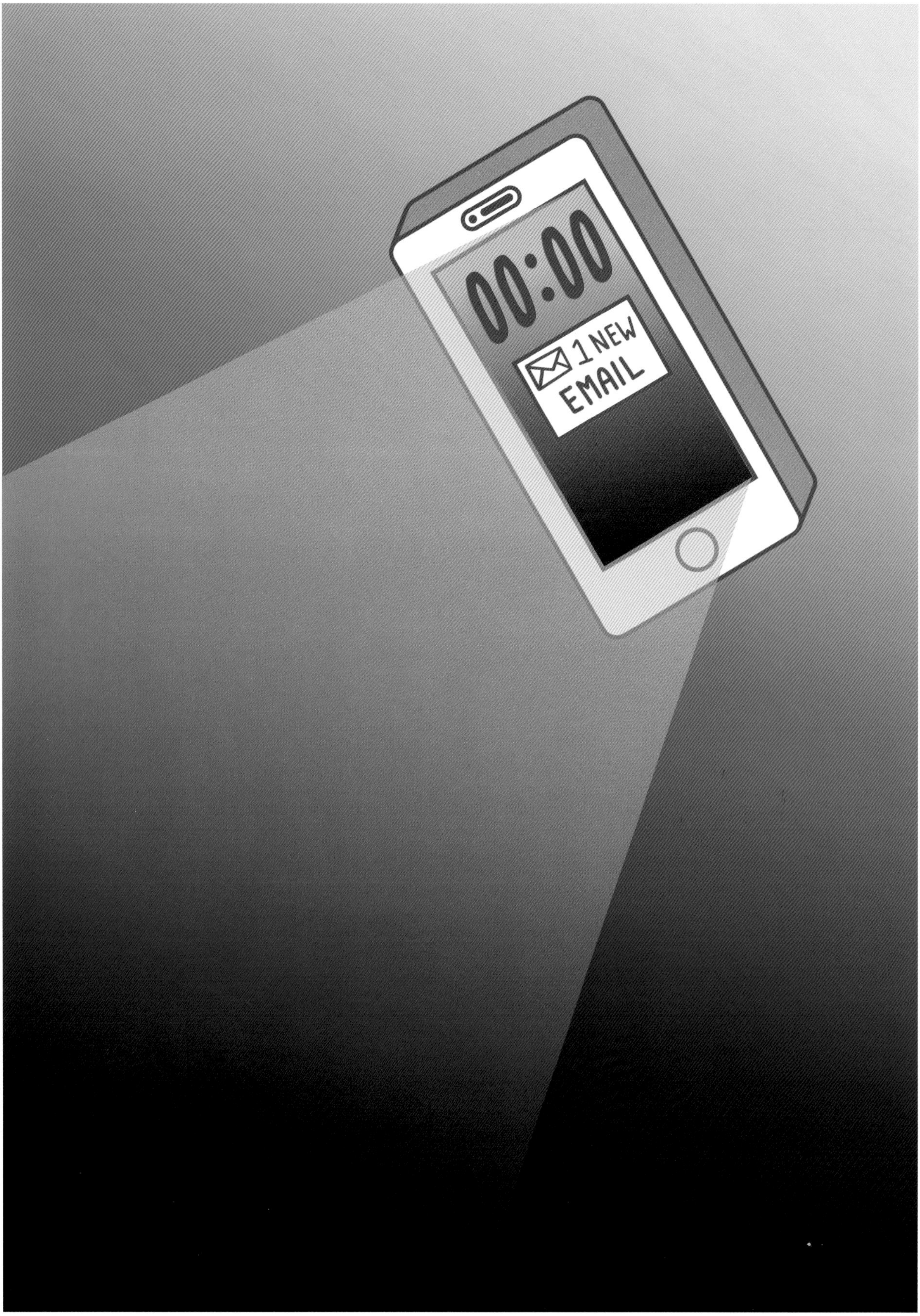
00:00
1 NEW EMAIL

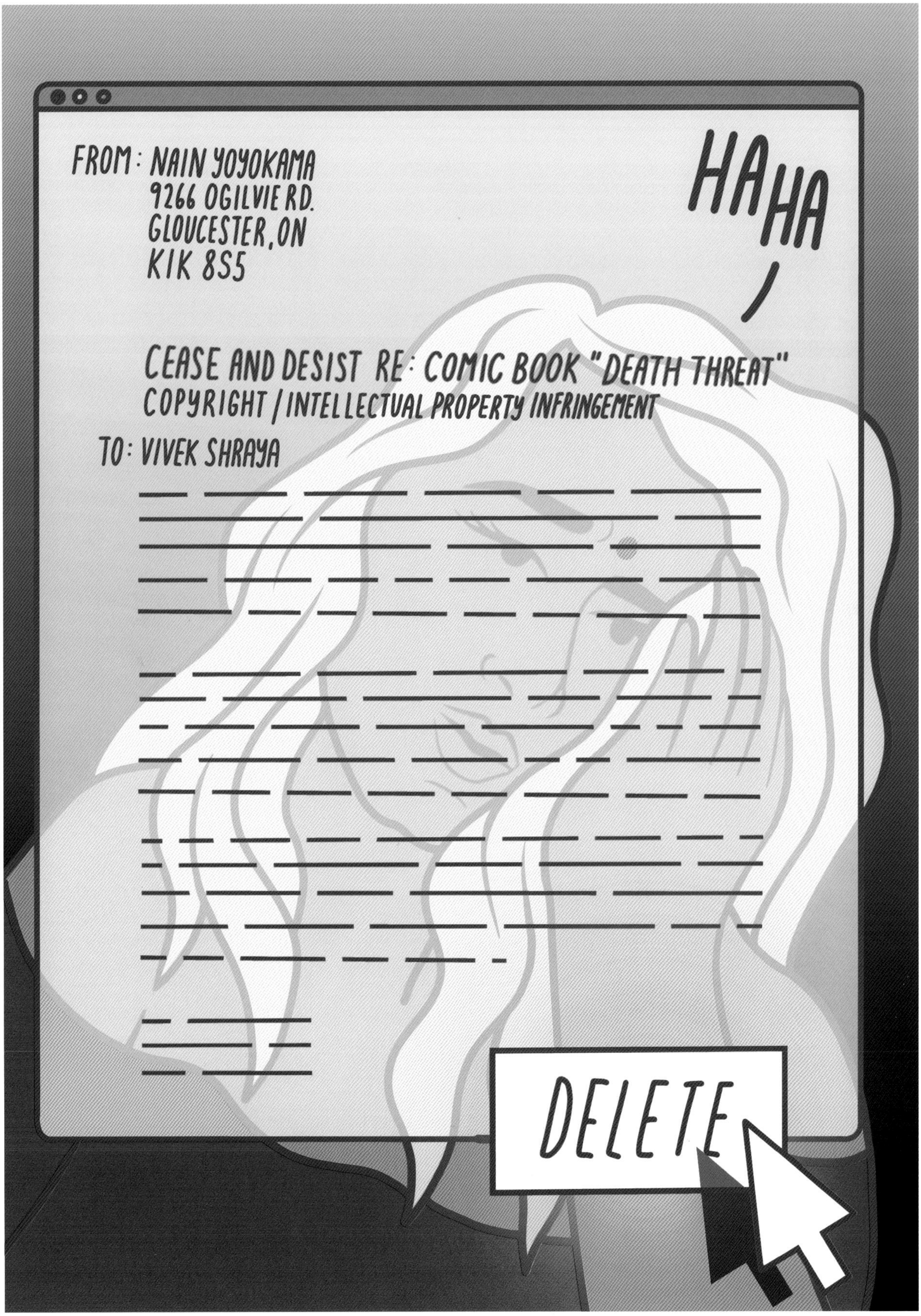
FROM: NAIN YOYOKAMA
9266 OGILVIE RD.
GLOUCESTER, ON
KIK 8S5
HAHAHA!
CEASE AND DESIST RE: COMIC BOOK "DEATH THREAT"
COPYRIGHT / INTELLECTUAL PROPERTY INFRINGEMENT
TO: VIVEK SHRAYA
DELETE

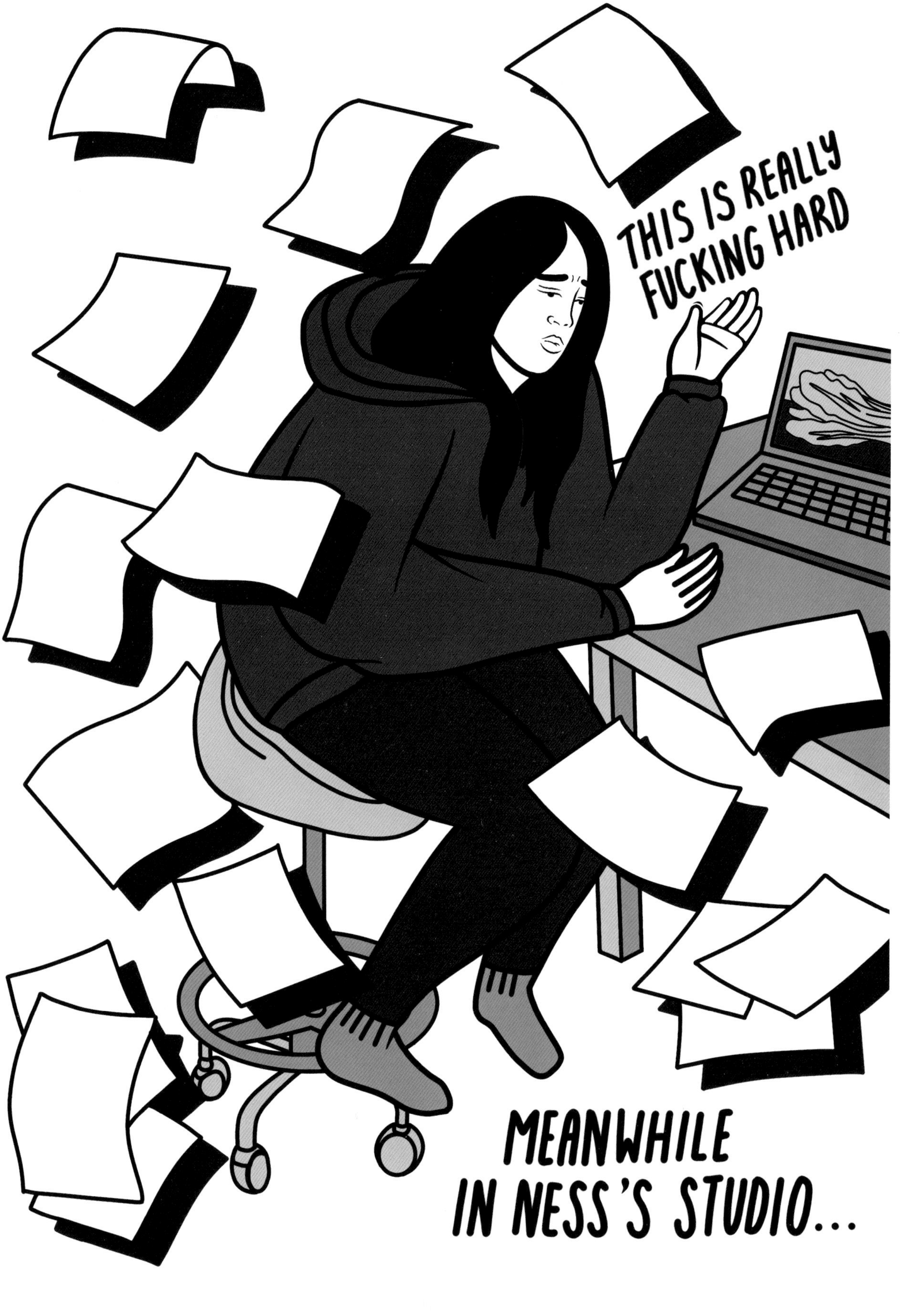
THIS IS REALLY FUCKING HARD
MEANWHILE IN NESS'S STUDIO...

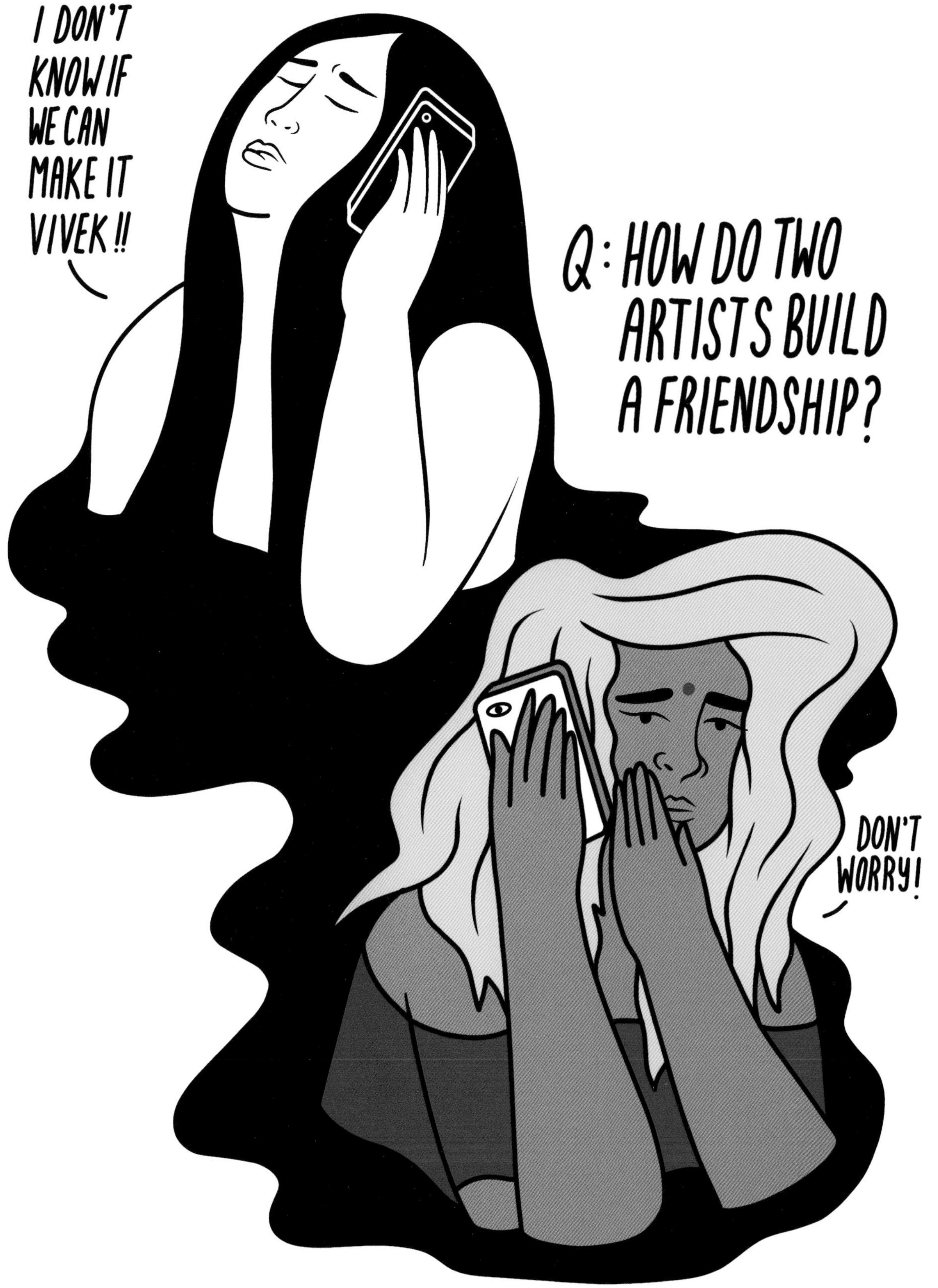
I DON'T KNOW IF WE CAN MAKE IT VIVEK !!
Q: HOW DO TWO ARTISTS BUILD A FRIENDSHIP?
DON'T WORRY!

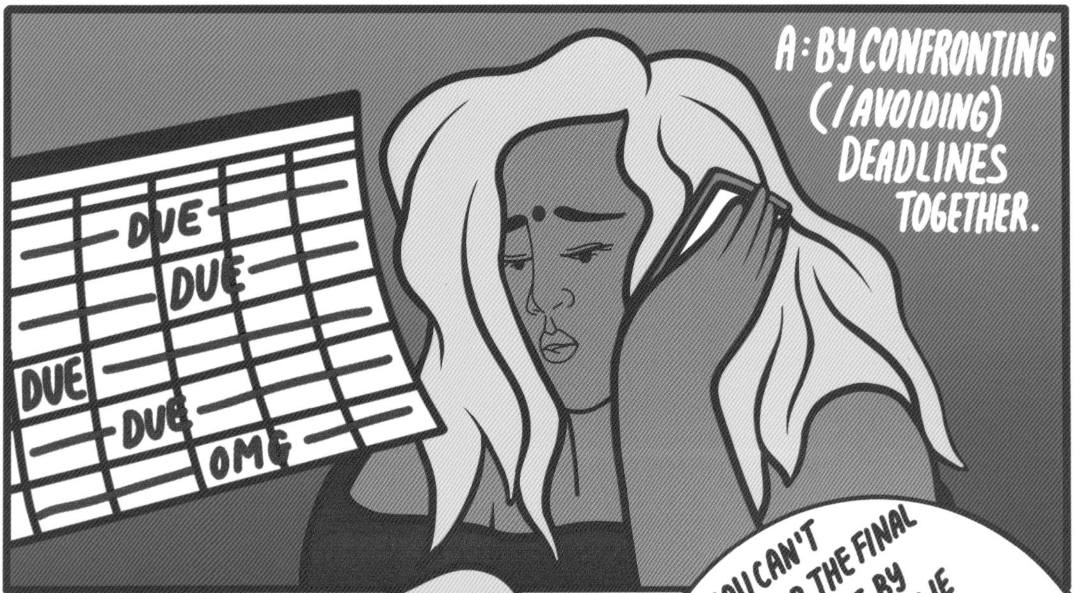
A: BY CONFRONTING (/AVOIDING) DEADLINES TOGETHER.
DUE
DUE
DUE
DUE
OMG

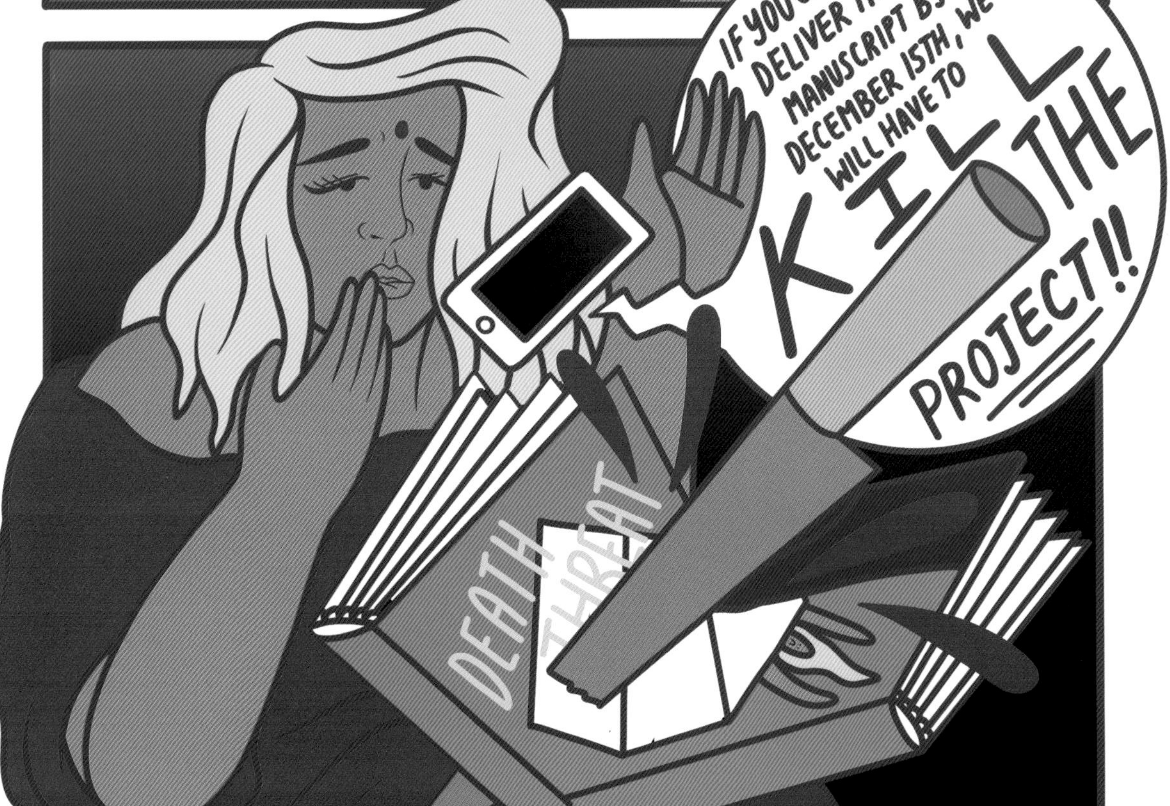
IF YOU CAN'T DELIVER THE FINAL MANUSCRIPT BY DECEMBER 15TH, WE WILL HAVE TO KILL THE PROJECT!!
DEATH THREAT

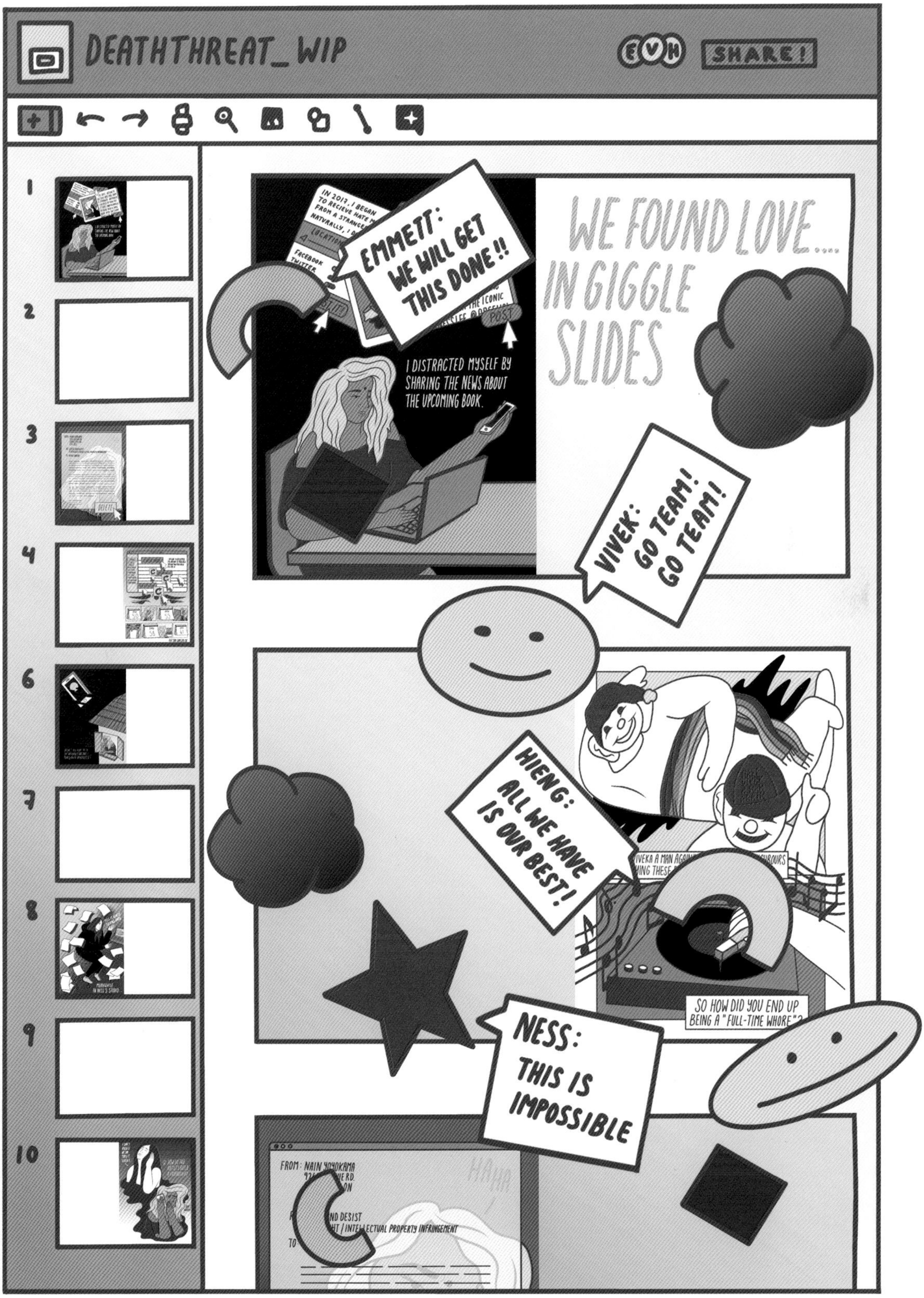

DEATHTHREAT_WIP
EVH
SHARE!
1
2
3
4
6
7
8
9
10
EMMETT: WE WILL GET THIS DONE!!
WE FOUND LOVE.... IN GIGGLE SLIDES
I DISTRACTED MYSELF BY SHARING THE NEWS ABOUT THE UPCOMING BOOK.
VIVEK: GO TEAM! GO TEAM!
HIENG: ALL WE HAVE IS OUR BEST!
SO HOW DID YOU END UP BEING A "FULL-TIME WHORE"?
NESS: THIS IS IMPOSSIBLE

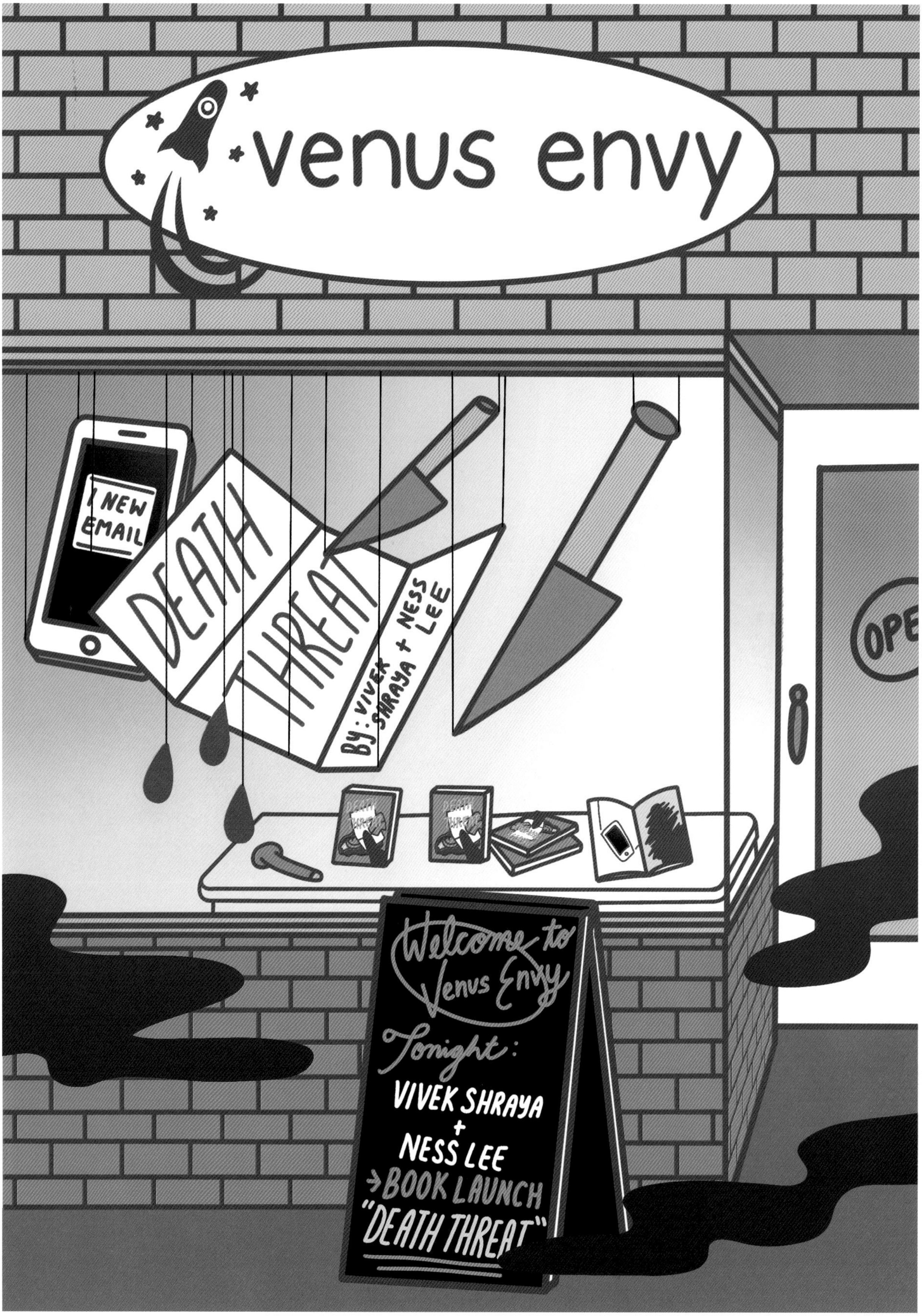
venus envy
1 NEW EMAIL
DEATH THREAT
BY: VIVEK SHRAYA + NESS LEE
OPE
Welcome to Venus Envy
Tonight:
VIVEK SHRAYA
+
NESS LEE
→BOOK LAUNCH
"DEATH THREAT"

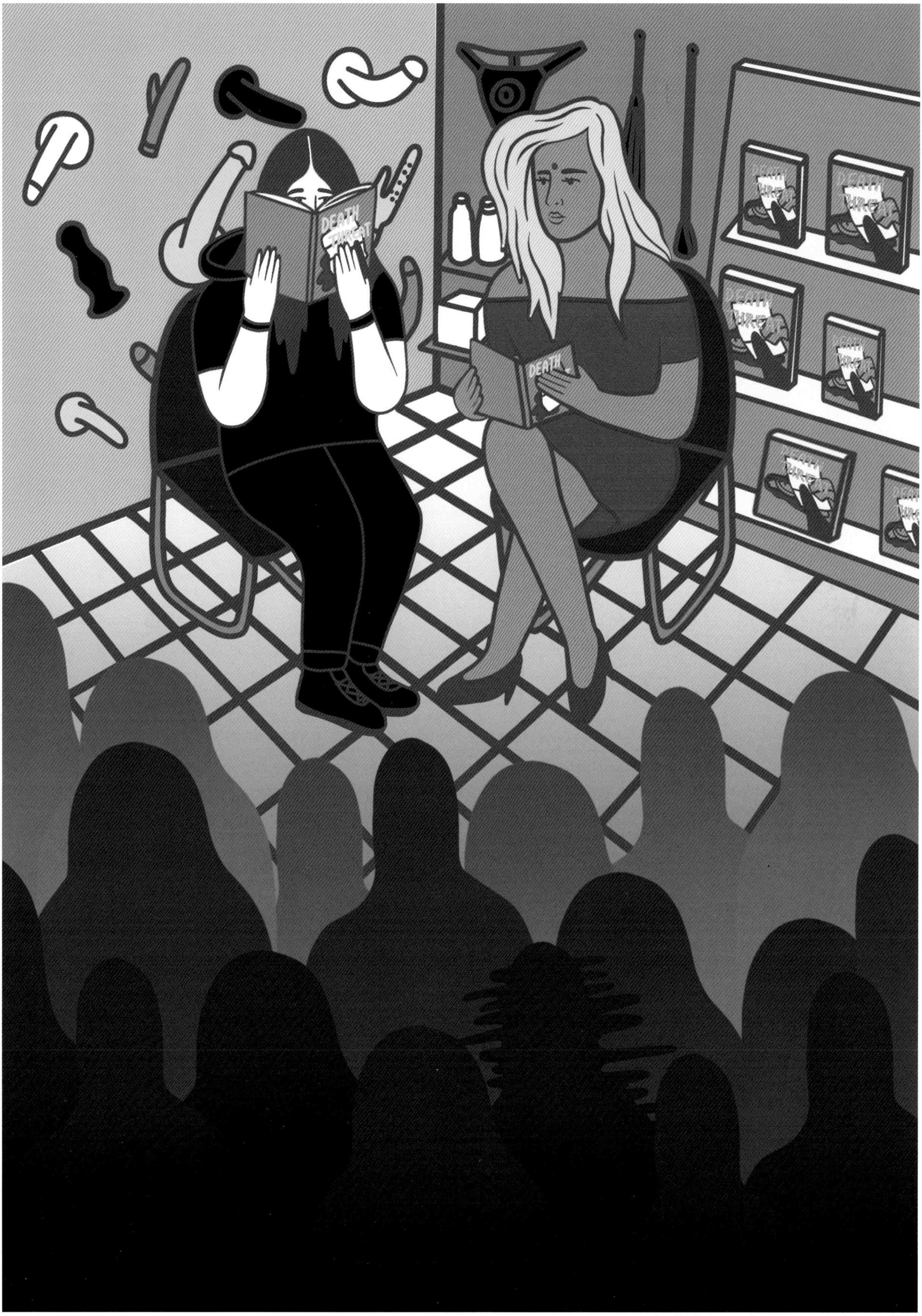
DEATH THREAT
DEATH

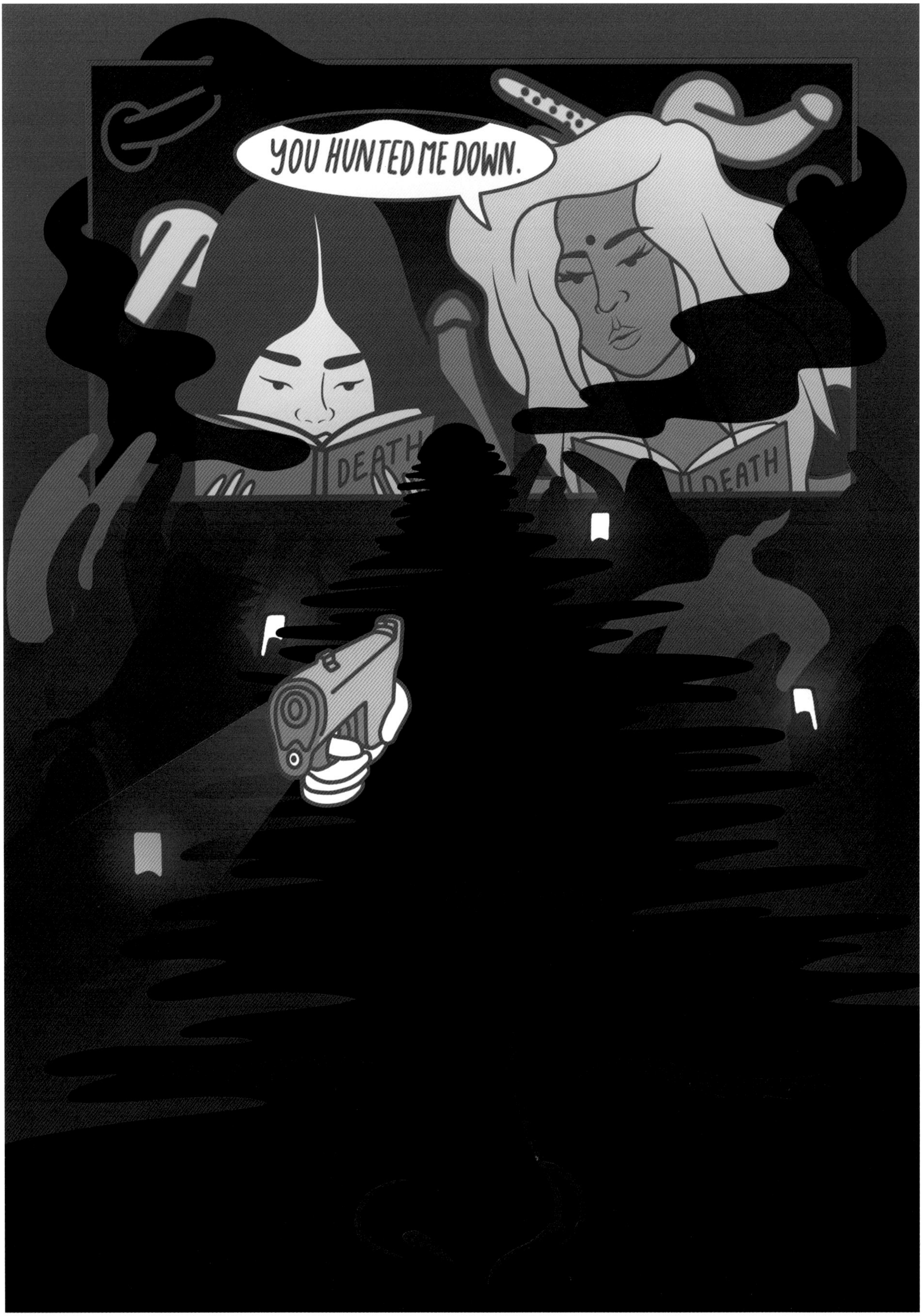
YOU HUNTED ME DOWN.
DEATH
DEATH

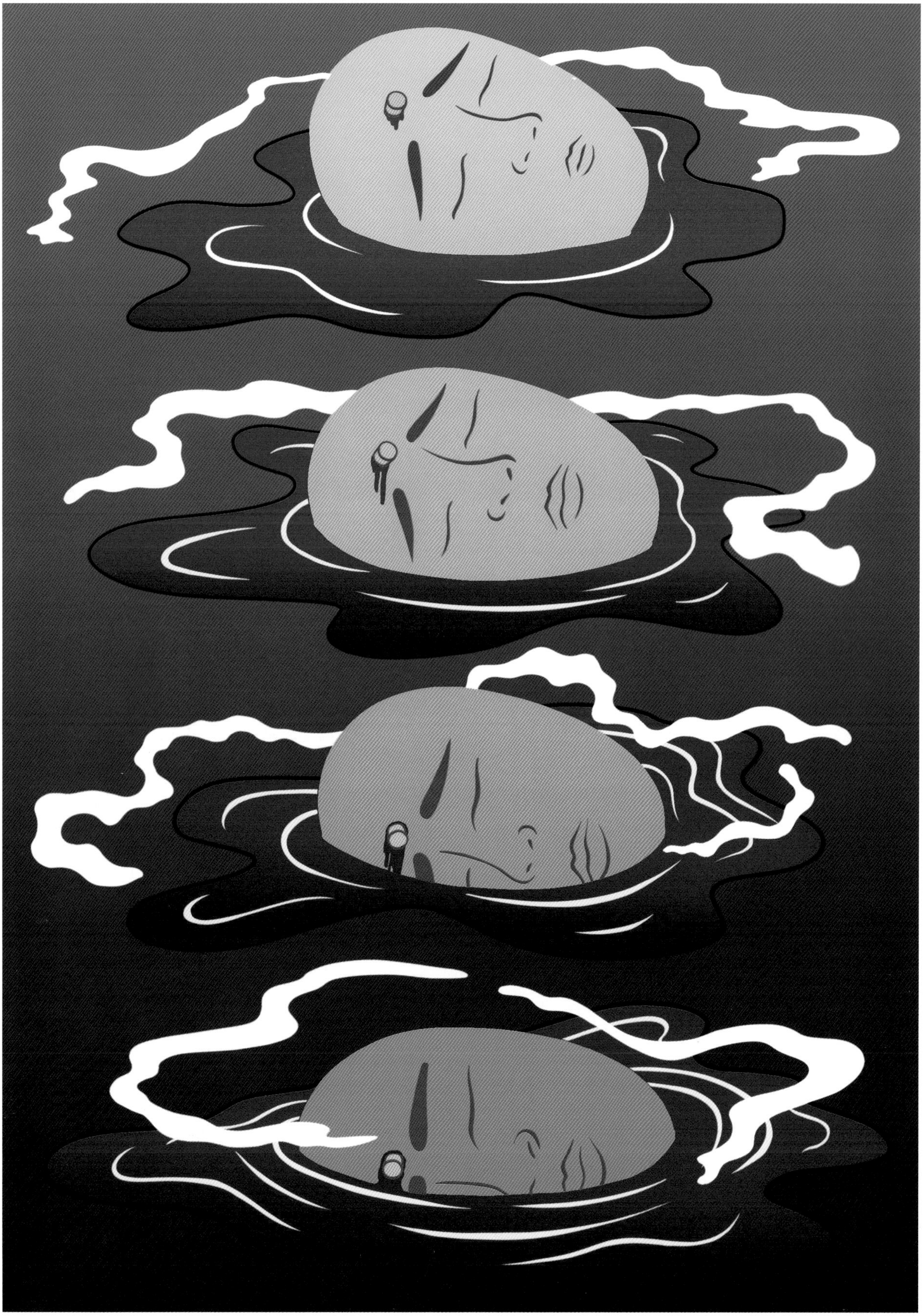

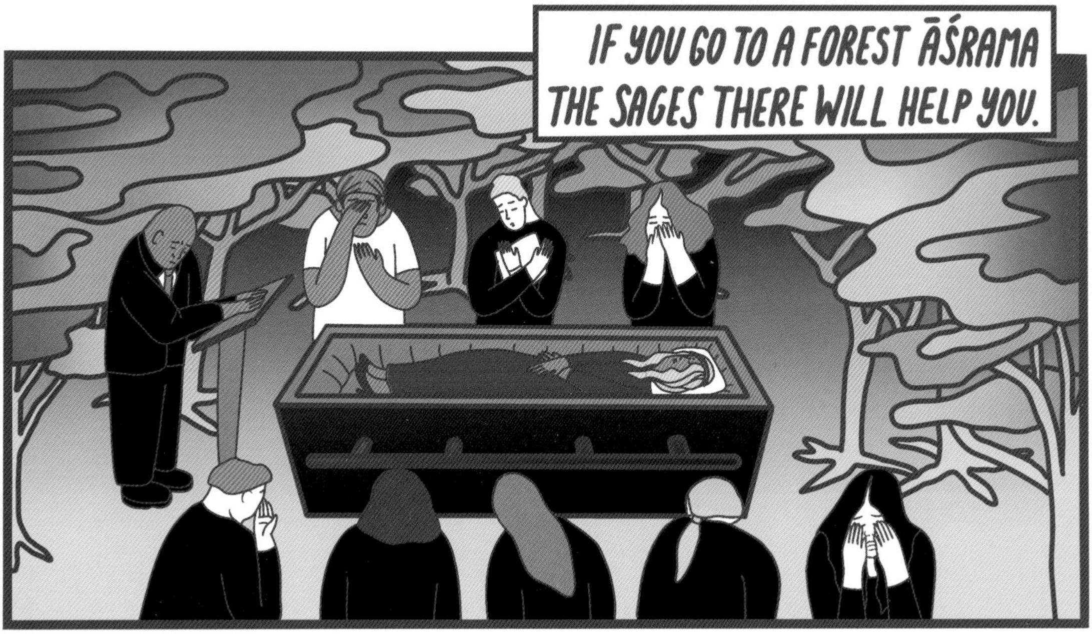
IF YOU GO TO A FOREST ĀŚRAMA THE SAGES THERE WILL HELP YOU.

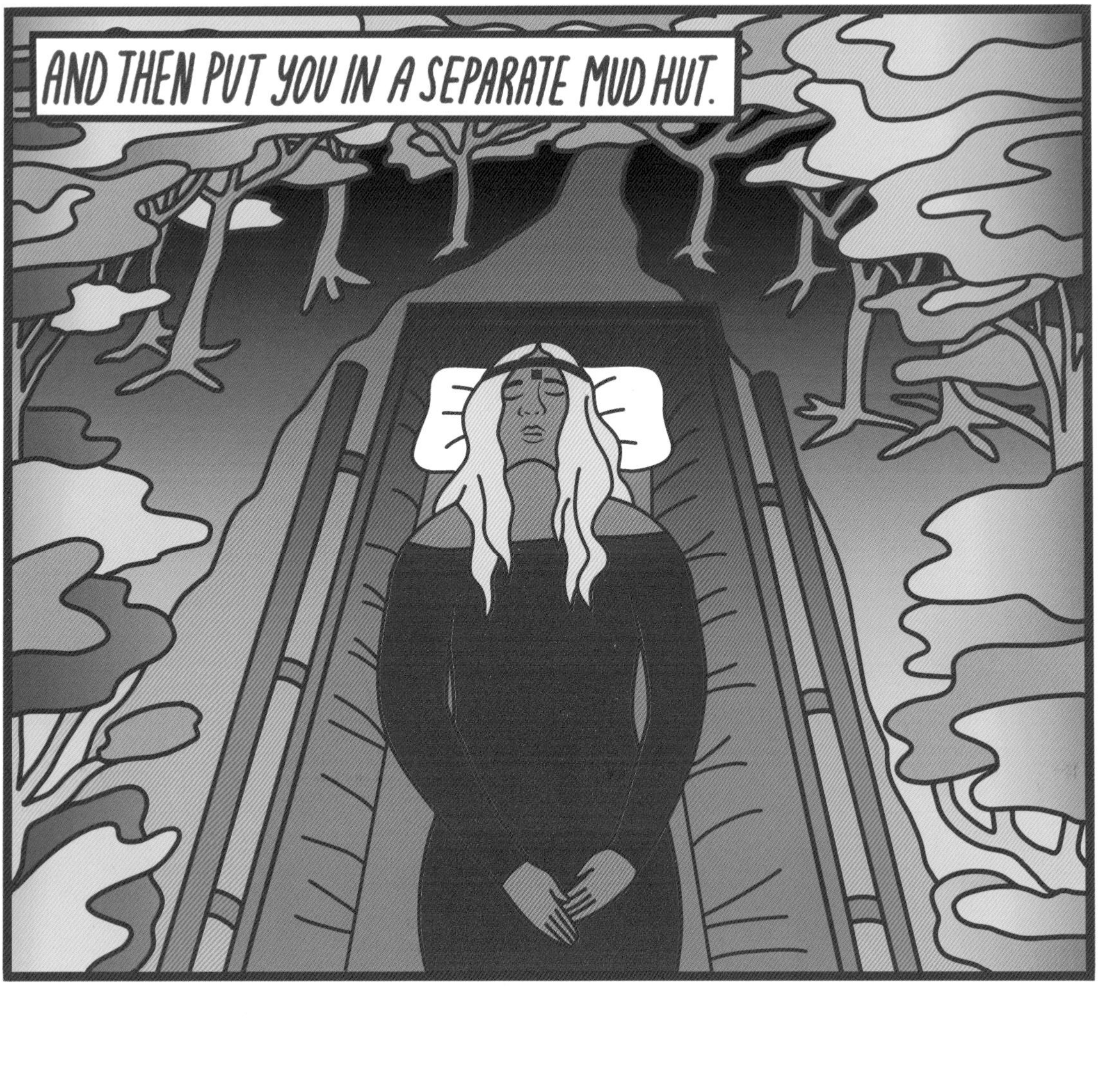
AND THEN PUT YOU IN A SEPARATE MUD HUT.

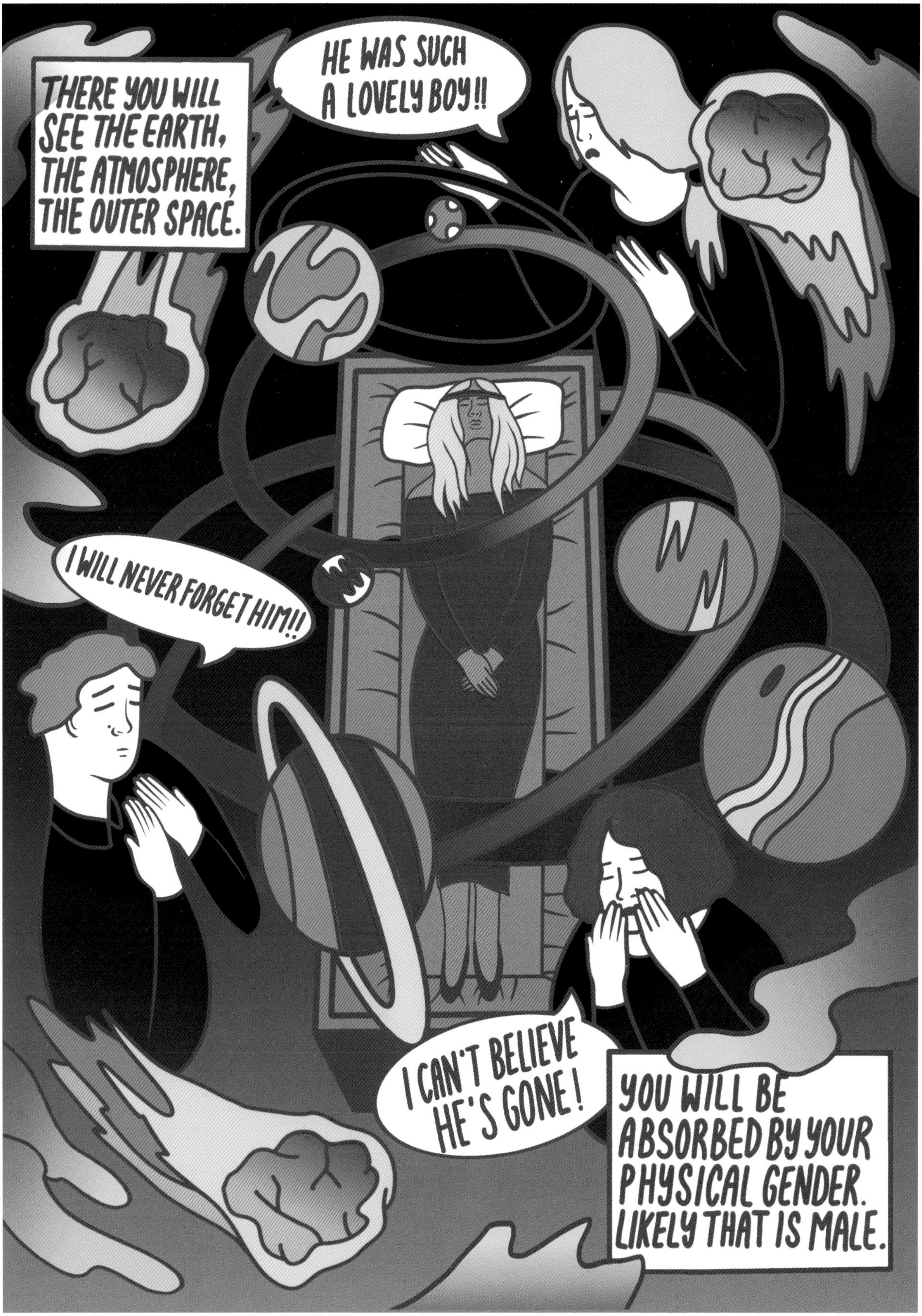
THERE YOU WILL SEE THE EARTH, THE ATMOSPHERE, THE OUTER SPACE.
HE WAS SUCH A LOVELY BOY!!
I WILL NEVER FORGET HIM!!
I CAN'T BELIEVE HE'S GONE!
YOU WILL BE ABSORBED BY YOUR PHYSICAL GENDER. LIKELY THAT IS MALE.

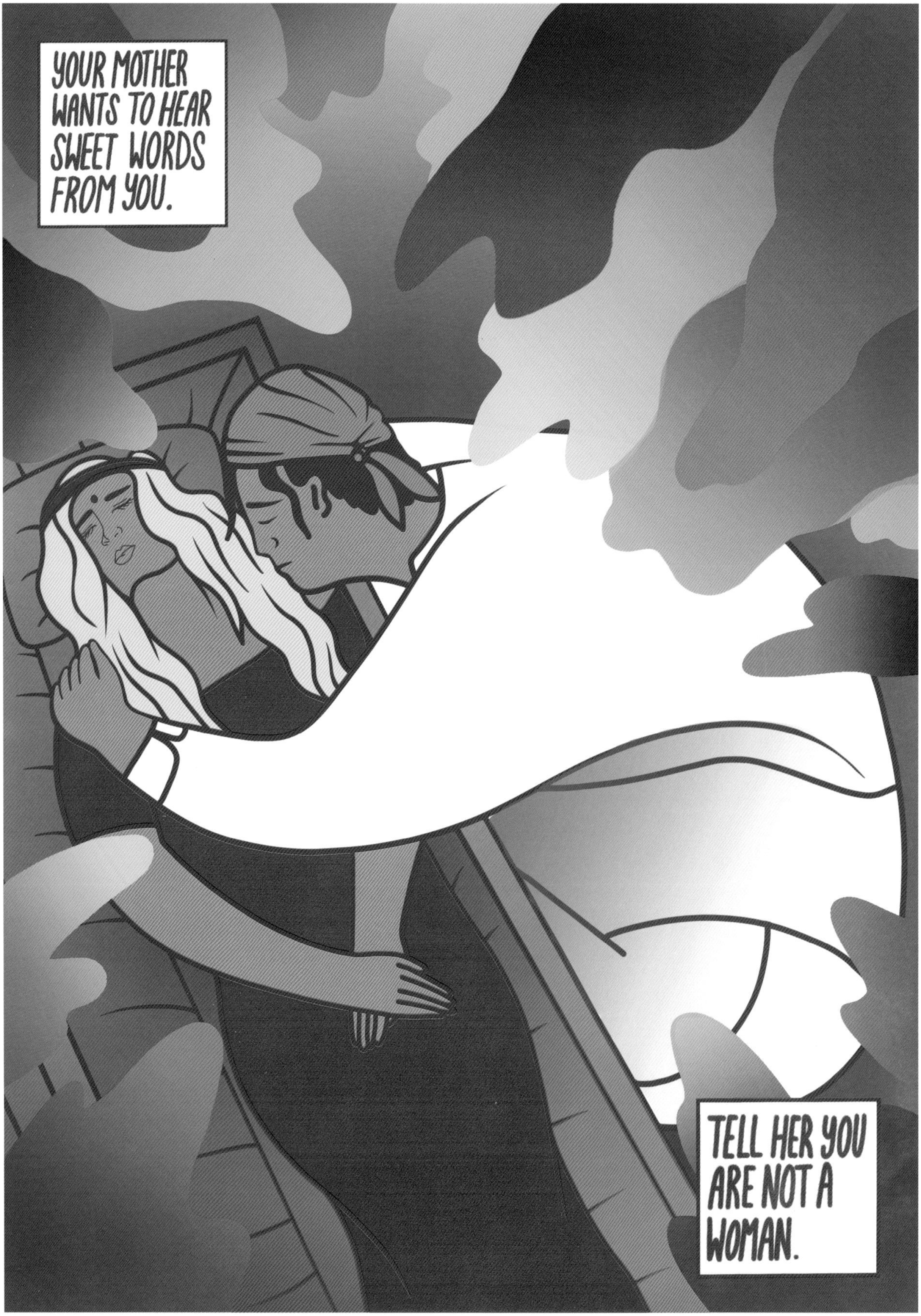
YOUR MOTHER WANTS TO HEAR SWEET WORDS FROM YOU.
TELL HER YOU ARE NOT A WOMAN.

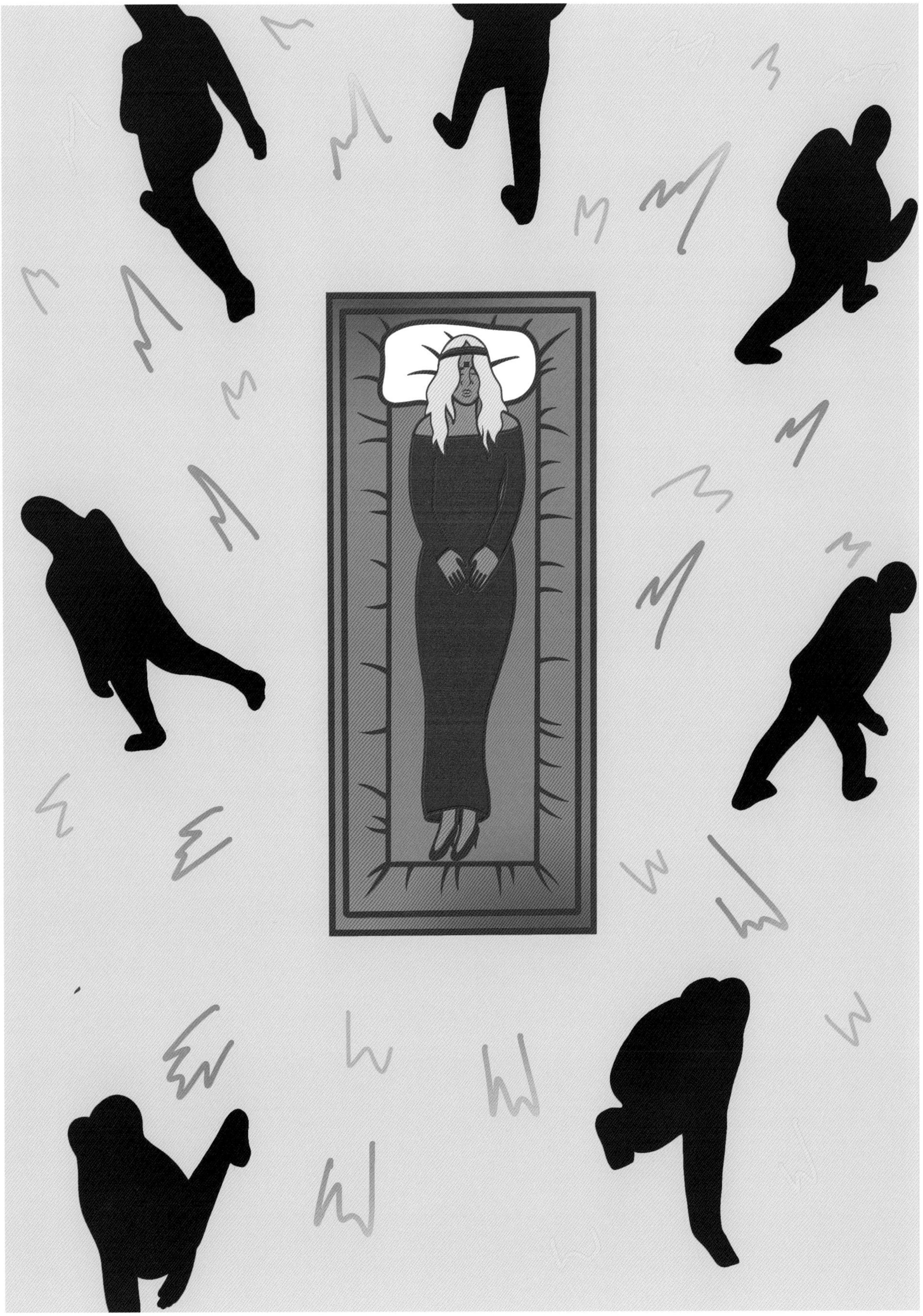

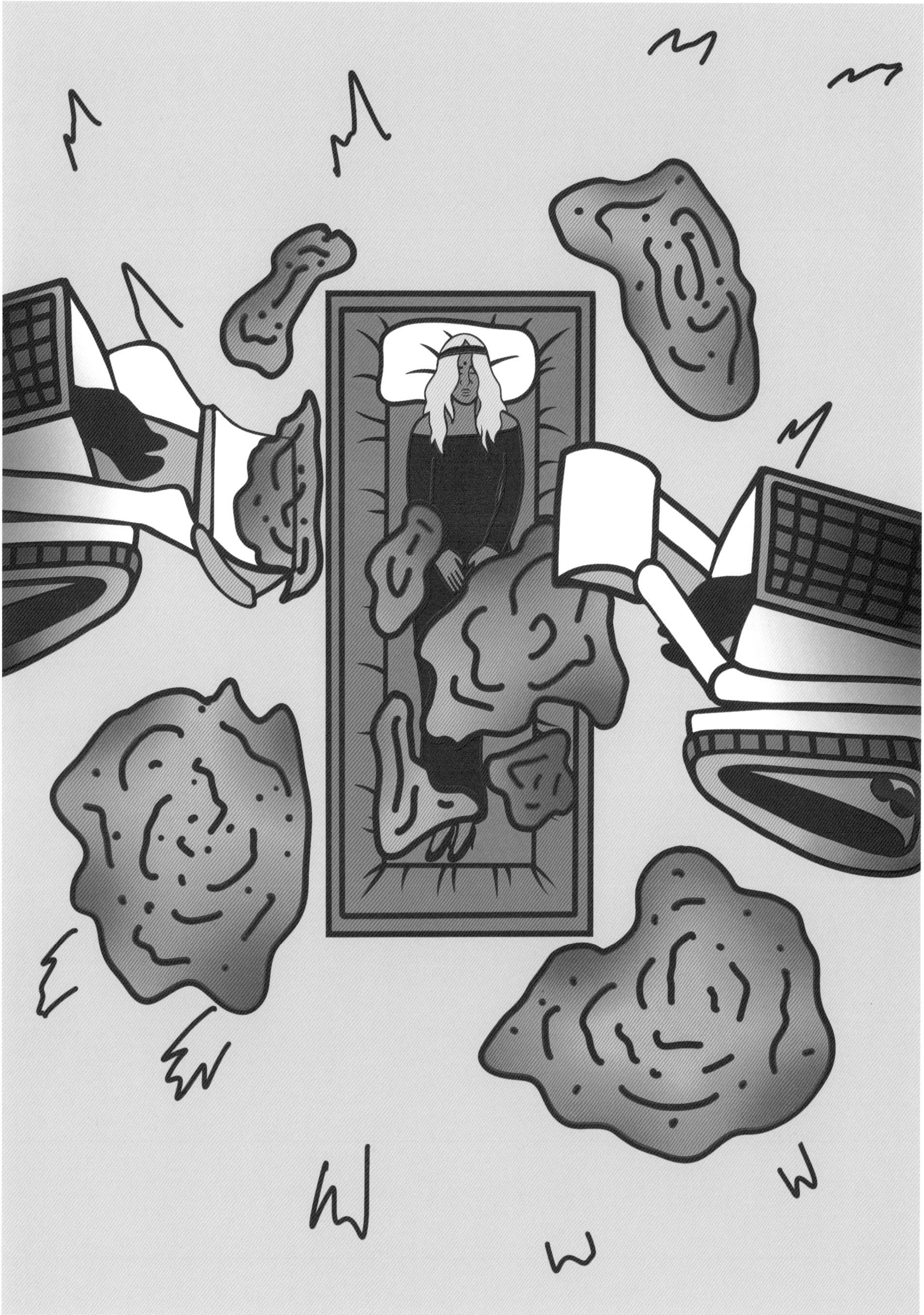

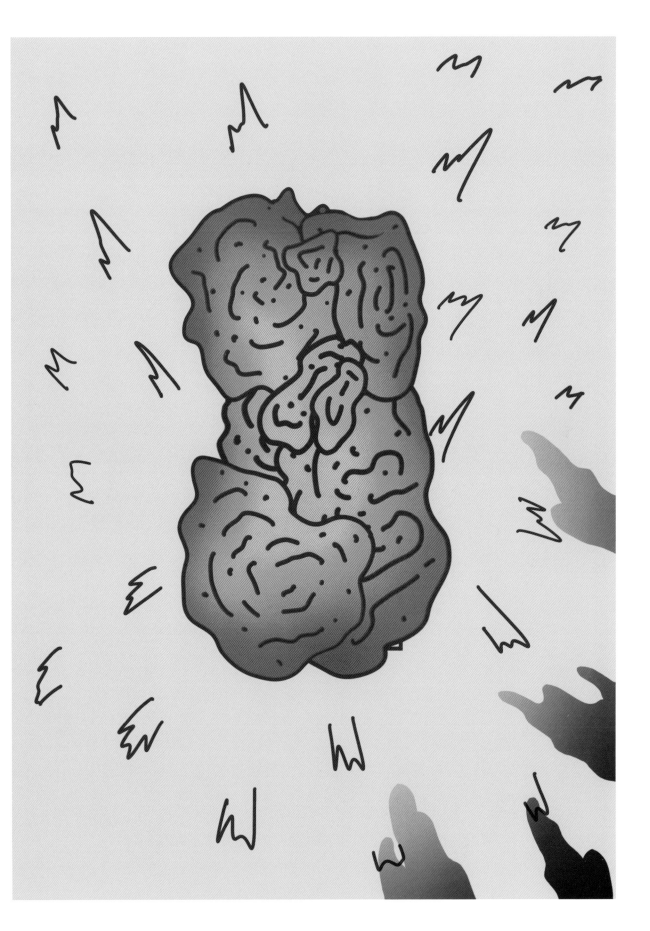

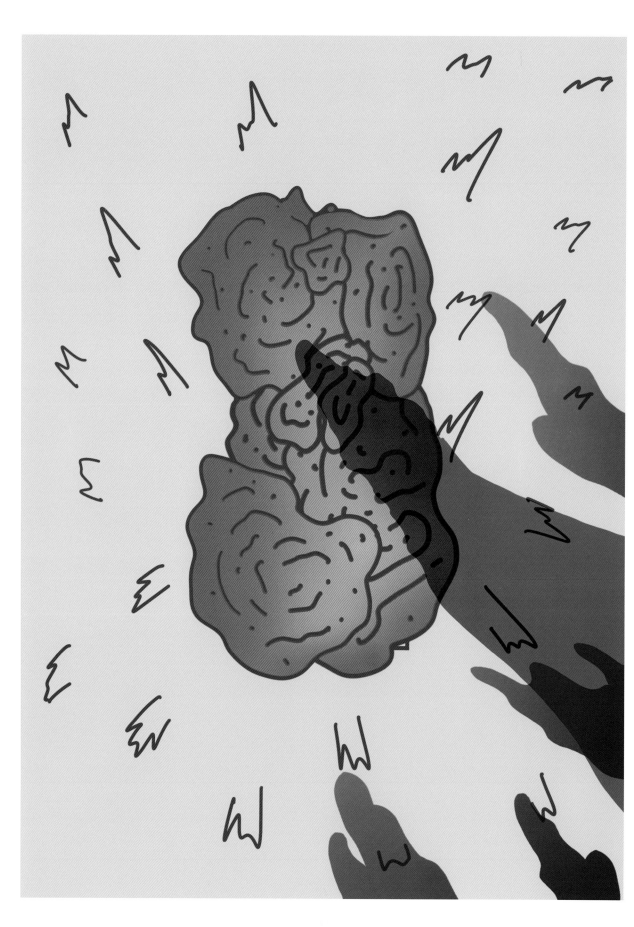

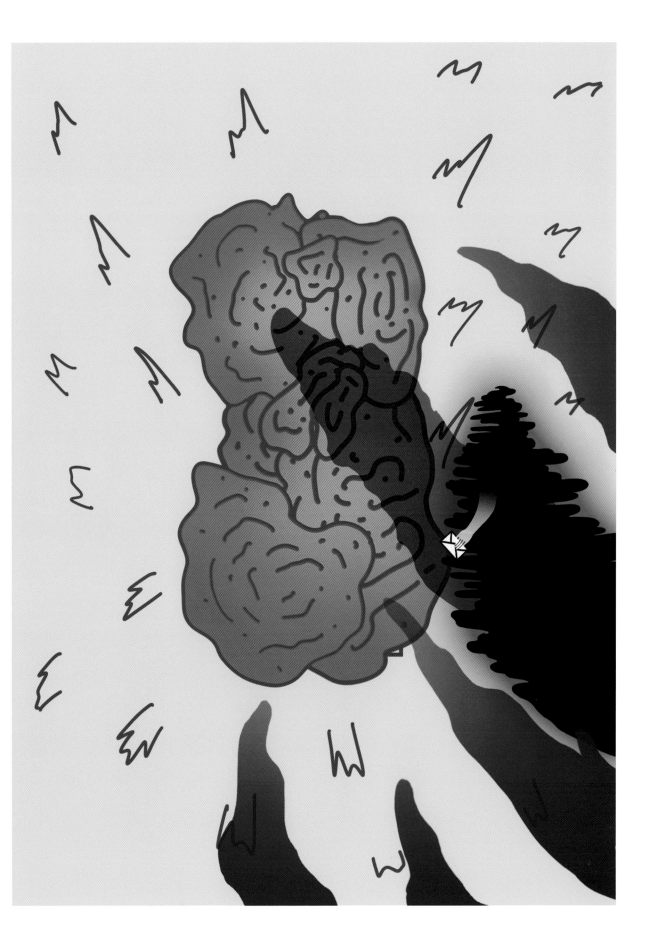

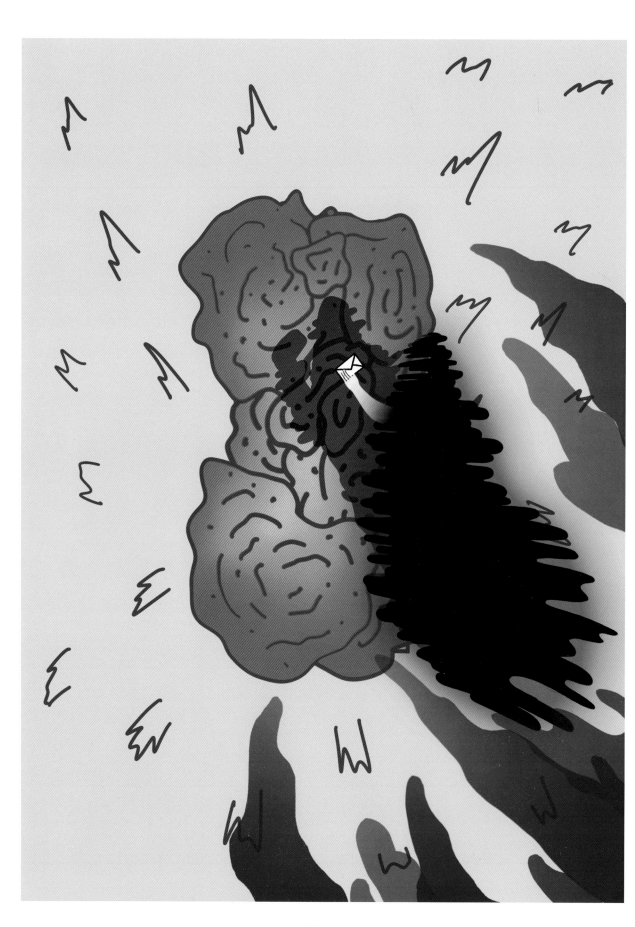

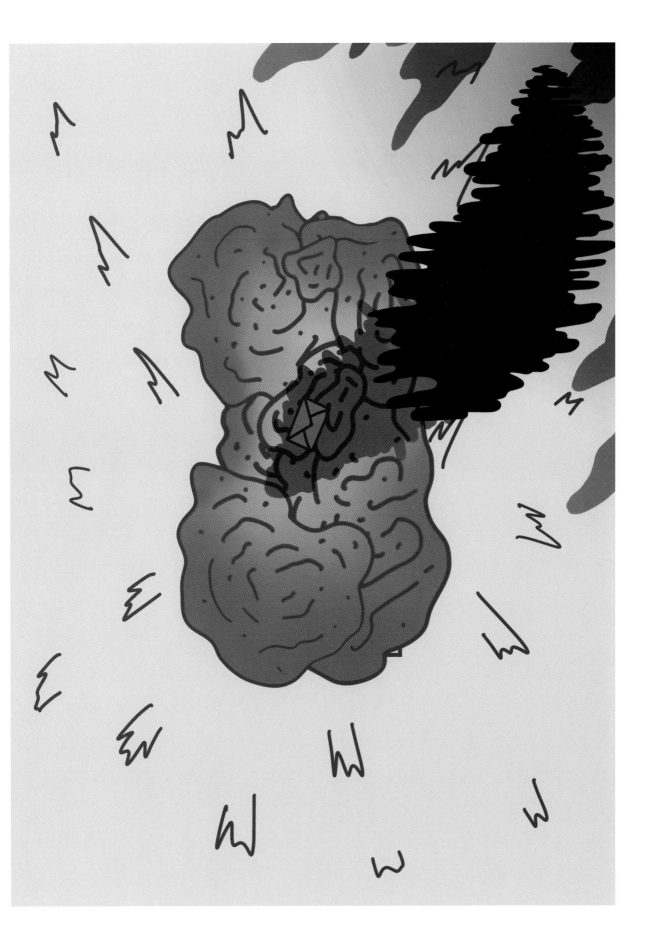

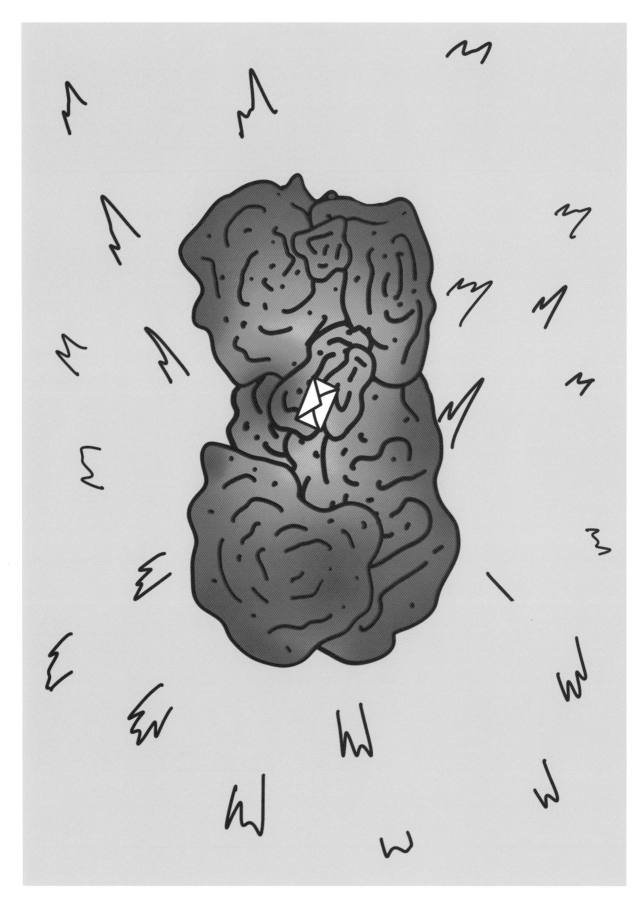

THE EXACT WORDING OF EMAILS FROM "NAIN" AND VIVEK'S MOM HAVE BEEN MOSTLY RETAINED IN ORDER TO MAINTAIN THIER VOICES.

VIVEK'S THANKS

AS SOMEONE WHO FIERCELY BELIEVES IN ATTRIBUTING CREDIT, I HAVE STRUGGLED WITH WRITING THESE ACKNOWLEDGMENTS — SPECIFICALLY, SHOULD I THANK "NAIN" FOR THIER MESSAGES? I AM NOT TYPICALLY INCLINED TO SHOW GRATITUDE FOR HATRED, SO INSTEAD I WILL THANK NESS LEE FOR BRILLIANTLY AND PATIENTLY TRANSFORMING HATE INTO ART, AND BRIAN LAM FOR GIVING THIS ART A HOME AT ARSENAL PULP PRESS.

THANK YOU, EMMETT PHAN AND HIENG TANG FOR BEING THE GREATEST AND MOST GENEROUS EMERGENCY COLOURISTS ON THE PLANET AND FOR REVIVING GRADIENTS.

THANK YOU TO MY MOM, ADAM HOLMAN, SHEMEENA SHRAYA, TALYA MACEDO, TRISHA YEO, AMBER DAWN, RACHEL LETOFSKY, JILLIAN TAMAKI, LISA HANAWALT, CYNARA GEISSLER, OLIVER MCPARTLIN, SHIRAROSE WILENSKY, SHAVONNE SOMVONG, SAMANTHA WHITTLE, AND VENUS ENVY OTTAWA.

ALSO GRATEFUL TO MICHELLE CAMPOS CASTILLO AND MICHAEL DEFORGE FOR USHERING ME INTO THE WORLD OF COMICS WITH THEIR ARTISTRY.

NESS'S THANKS

THIS COMIC WOULDN'T HAVE MADE IT TO THE END (LET ALONE EXIST) WITHOUT THE CONSTANT CARE, SUPPORT, AND ENCOURAGING BELIEF THAT VIVEK SHRAYA HAS HAD FOR ME IN THIS PROCESS. TO BE ABLE TO SHARE THIS EXPERIENCE TOGETHER, FOR HER TO OPEN HER WORLD AND STORY TO ME WITH SUCH PATIENCE, FAITH, AND CREATIVE FREEDOM, IS A FEELING I WILL NEVER FORGET.

I HAVE THE BIGGEST LOVE FOR EMMETT PHAN AND HIENG TANG— FOR WITHOUT THESE TWO, THIS COMIC WOULD LITERALLY NOT BE COMPLETE. THANK YOU FOR SHOWING UP, BEING THERE, AND TEACHING ME, ALWAYS.

THANK YOU, ARSENAL PULP PRESS FAMILY FOR THE ENDLESS PATIENCE—FOR WELCOMING THIS COMIC INTO EXISTENCE, AND THE ENDLESS AMOUNT OF WORK THAT IS REQUIRED TO MANAGE ALL THE MOVING PARTS OF CONCEIVING A BOOK AND LAUNCHING ITS LIFE INTO THE WORLD.

THANK YOU TO MOM AND DAD, LIONEL, KISUNG KOH, KATE KWON, AMY GREENWOOD, POE, RENZO, TABBAN SOLEIMANI, MELISSA LUK, DEVAN PATEL, TESSAR LO, AYA HIGASHITSUGI-LO, CHRISTINA THAI, GRACE THAI, JENNIFER THAI AND ERIC LO.

GRATEFUL FOR JILLIAN TAMAKI, MICHAEL DEFORGE, AND LISA HANAWALT—THANK YOU SO MUCH!!

VIVEK SHRAYA IS AN ARTIST WHOSE BODY OF WORK CROSSES THE BOUNDARIES OF MUSIC, LITERATURE, VISUAL ART, AND FILM. HER BEST-SELLING BOOK *I'M AFRAID OF MEN* WAS HERALDED BY *VANITY FAIR* AS "CULTURAL ROCKET FUEL," AND HER ALBUM *PART-TIME WOMAN*, WITH QUEER SONGBOOK ORCHESTRA, WAS INCLUDED IN CBC'S LIST OF BEST CANADIAN ALBUMS OF 2017. SHE IS ONE HALF OF THE MUSIC DUO TOO ATTACHED AND THE FOUNDER OF THE PUBLISHING IMPRINT VS. BOOKS. A POLARIS MUSIC PRIZE NOMINEE AND FOUR-TIME LAMBDA LITERARY AWARD FINALIST, VIVEK WAS A 2016 PRIDE TORONTO GRAND MARSHAL, WAS FEATURED ON *THE GLOBE AND MAIL'S* BEST DRESSED LIST, AND HAS RECEIVED HONOURS FROM THE WRITERS' TRUST OF CANADA AND THE PUBLISHING TRIANGLE. SHE IS A DIRECTOR ON THE BOARD OF THE TEGAN AND SARA FOUNDATION AND AN ASSISTANT PROFESSOR OF CREATIVE WRITING AT THE UNIVERSITY OF CALGARY.
VIVEKSHRAYA.COM / @VIVEKSHRAYA

NESS LEE IS AN ILLUSTRATOR AND ARTIST BASED IN TKARONTO/TORONTO, CANADA. HER ILLUSTRATIONS HAVE BEEN CHOSEN FOR AWARD PUBLICATIONS SUCH AS *AMERICAN ILLUSTRATION 35* AND *SOCIETY OF ILLUSTRATORS 57*, AND SHE HAS EXHIBITED HER WORKS AT GALLERIES IN TORONTO, NEW YORK, BOSTON, LOS ANGELES AND TOKYO. SHE CONTINUES TO EXPLORE HER PRACTICE USING A WIDE RANGE OF MEDIUMS SUCH AS CERAMICS, DRAWING, PAINTING, MIXED MEDIA, AND SCULPTURE.
NESSLEE.COM / @NESSLEEE

ARSENAL PULP PRESS
SUITE 202-211 EAST GEORGIA ST.
VANCOUVER, BC V6A 1Z6
CANADA
ARSENALPULP.COM

THE PUBLISHER GRATEFULLY ACKNOWLEDGES THE SUPPORT OF THE CANADA COUNCIL FOR THE ARTS AND THE BRITISH COLUMBIA ARTS COUNCIL FOR ITS PUBLISHING PROGRAM, AND THE GOVERNMENT OF CANADA, AND THE GOVERNMENT OF BRITISH COLUMBIA (THROUGH THE BOOK PUBLISHING TAX CREDIT PROGRAM), FOR ITS PUBLISHING ACTIVITES.

British Columbia | British Columbia Arts Council — An agency of the Province of British Columbia | Canada Council for the Arts | Conseil des arts du Canada | Canada

ARSENAL PULP PRESS ACKNOWLEDGES THE XʷMƎΘKʷƎYƎM (MUSQUEAM), SKWXWÚ7MESH (SQUAMISH), AND SƎL̓ÍLWƎTAʔɬ (TSLEIL-WAUTUTH) NATIONS, SPEAKERS OF HUL̓Q̓UMI̓NUM̓ / HALQ̓EMÉYLEM / HƎN̓Q̓ƎMIN̓ƎM̓ AND CUSTODIANS OF THE TRADITIONAL, ANCESTRAL, AND UNCEDED TERRITORIES WHERE OUR OFFICE IS LOCATED. WE PAY RESPECT TO THEIR HISTORIES, TRADITIONS, AND CONTINUOUS LIVING CULTURES AND COMMIT TO ACCOUNTABILITY, RESPECTFUL RELATIONS, AND FRIENDSHIP.

PRINTED AND BOUND IN CANADA

LIBRARY AND ARCHIVES CANADA CATALOGUING IN PUBLICATION:

SHRAYA, VIVEK, 1981-, AUTHOR

DEATH THREAT / VIVEK SHRAYA + NESS LEE.

ISSUED IN PRINT AND ELECTRONIC FORMATS.

ISBN 978-1-55152-750-5 (HARDCOVER)—ISBN 978-1-55152-751-2 (PDF)

1. TRANSPHOBIA—COMIC BOOKS, STRIPS, ETC. 2. TRANSGENDER PEOPLE—CRIMES AGAINST—COMIC BOOKS, STRIPS, ETC. 3. HATE MAIL—COMIC BOOKS, STRIPS, ETC. 4. ANONYMOUS LETTERS—COMIC BOOKS, STRIPS, ETC. 5. GRAPHIC NOVELS. I. LEE, NESS, ILLUSTRATOR II. TITLE.

HQ77.96.S47 2019 306.76'8 C2018-906212-6
C2018-906213-4